RETURNING WHAT'S SACRED

A True Story By
MARIE DION

Edited and Encouraged by Charisse Sisou

Copyright ©2025 Marie Dion

Disclaimer | RETURNING WHAT'S SACRED

What you're about to read is my truth and my experience alone. This is my recollection of events, which I have related to the best of my knowledge. Names, identities, and other related information have been changed or are a composite to protect people's privacy. The way this book came through me, my past life memories, visions and experiences, and the information from Spirit is for you to believe or not. In sharing what I have, my hope is that others learn to trust themselves and their own journey in life, to have a sense of hope, and to get to a better place within themselves, a place of understanding and peace.

Copyright ©2025 Marie Dion.

All rights reserved. No part of this book may be used or reproduced by any means, graphic, electronic, or mechanical, including photocopying, recording, taping or by any information storage retrieval system without the written permission of the author except in the case of brief quotations embodied in critical articles and reviews.

All the photography, and artwork are my own and may not be reproduced in any form, print or digital, without written permission.
Copyright Holder: Marie Dion

Because of the dynamic nature of the Internet, any web addresses or links contained in this book may have changed since publication and may no longer be valid.

To order additional copies of *Returning What's Sacred*, visit mariedion.com.

ISBN: 978-1-7329035-4-8

"She is the truth teller, maybe that people hate to hear,
but they learn to listen to."

—Dr. Clarissa Pinkola Estes

WHAT PEOPLE ARE SAYING

"This book allows the reader to see that any act they have done, whether large or small, can impact the rest of the world and humanity. Everyone can see themselves in your story and that their struggle is just as important as everybody else's. It gives people hope and lets them know that they are not alone. By being led by complete faith to get through it all, you give the reader hope, even if they can't hear their ancestors. Tuning into the unseen, everybody has access to this. Look and listen, the signs are all around us. It takes so much courage to live in faith. This book is needed now because courage is needed now."

—Sandi Isgro, *President, American Society of Dowsers*

"Chills. It's 3:30 am, I need to go to bed but instead I'm crying and wanting to continue reading. This story is a blessing in itself. The impact this has on me, as a person who is walking the [red] road, provides a healing in a way I can't fully explain. *Standing ovation.* This book is truth and faith. It will not be an easy read for most but the people who read this book will be impacted physically, emotionally, mentally and spiritually in a conscious and unconscious way. As I read this book my heart ached, cried and rejoiced for you and with you. You have healed all of us in different ways, and for that, every piece of my soul thanks you. I can't explain to you in full words the impact and emotions I feel right now, but just know the ripple effect will be beyond your comprehension in the best way possible. Kuttabotomish. You have and always will be a gift to me and every person you meet."

—Willow Daly, *Nipmuc Tribal citizen, Ohketeau; Coordinator, Eastern Woodlands Rematriation*

DEDICATION

For those who are the seventh generation, indigenous or not…

For our ancestors who prayed for this day…

For Grandfather, who guided the journey.

And for White Wolf, may the rest of your journey be at peace.

FOREWORD
by Charisse Sisou

How does one return what's sacred? And beyond that, how do we return *to* the sacred?

Returning What's Sacred by Marie Dion flies like the tip of an arrow straight to the heart of why these questions matter now.

Marie Dion's *Returning What's Sacred* poses these questions literally and spiritually. She embarks on an epic journey to return a sacred item to its ancestral home—and shows us, through her lived experience, what it means to walk in harmony with the unseen, guided by Spirit and trusting in Creator.

As a First Nations woman healing land, lineage, and lifetimes, Marie confronts the omissions of textbook history and remembers what has been erased. How do we say what's true when the victor writes history? When what is "sacred" means different things to different people?

And how do we build a future together, if not by remembering what once sustained us, and honoring all perspectives?

The author shows us how, step by step, moment by moment. Mundane and transcendent.

We are, collectively, in a time of returning what's sacred and

Foreword | Returning What's Sacred

reintegrating original ways of knowing and being.

Marie's story reveals that restoring a sacred item or honoring holy ground is not a solitary act. It is a ripple that heals generations, releasing history's grip on the land. With wisdom and humor, she shows us that we can correct past wrongs with love and compassion—and that anyone can do this work when called to heal their lineage, history, and environment.

As Dion writes, she shares her story so we might better understand our own. So we, too, can remember how to live in step with Spirit—and what happens when we allow ourselves to trust.

Each of us carries a piece of the medicine of this healing. (You wouldn't be holding this book otherwise.) Our ancestors bore their part, even through sacrifice, survival, and surrender.

Every time we step toward reconciliation, as in Marie's heartfelt journey, we change the human tapestry. Native peoples have long called for the return of stolen artifacts. As you'll see, returning even one can create seismic ripples across lives and communities.

This book is for those still fighting for land, life, and sacred inheritance, and the people who support them. For the Sioux and 200+ tribes who stood at Standing Rock. For Native Hawaiians, protecting Mauna Kea. For Indigenous land defenders in the Philippines, risking everything. And so many more, often excluded from mainstream coverage.

Returning What's Sacred reminds us that even when the challenges seem insurmountable, there is a way through: the humble choices of individuals. The courage to say yes, even when we're scared, or unsure—or end up in totally unfamiliar territory, like Marie!

It's been my great honor to walk this path with the author, translating her memories, stories, and channels into the book you now read. With reverence, I thank the wisdom keepers who made this book possible. Who, when it was forbidden, prayed in secret, hid their ceremonies, and whispered their language in their children's ears, so the sacred thread could be carried forward. The grandmothers and grandfathers whose sacrifices and prayers made it possible for Marie to tell her story—and for us to benefit from it.

In *Returning What's Sacred*, Marie Dion invites us to glimpse what's possible when we remember what we once knew: to live in step with Spirit, the Earth, and each other, and in so doing, heal ourselves, reconcile, and reimagine our future.

Thank you, Marie, for trusting us with your story. May its ripple be felt far and wide.

With love,
Charisse Sisou
Author and Host of *Wise Body, Ancient Soul*

Introduction | Returning What's Sacred

INTRODUCTION

For those of the seventh generation, an awakening is happening across the globe. Indigenous or not, people are remembering. And some, like me, are born remembering.

My ancestors insisted that this book be written. As much as I tried not to write it, I had to. This is my story and mine alone, and I am telling it in the way it happened to me. Though to some, my life seems extraordinary, it is my everyday experience. I am guided by my ancestors in all that I do, from the mundane to the not-so.

The experiences I share in this book happened from 2019 to 2025, unfolding moment by moment. Whether it helps people heal, awaken, understand, or simply touches your heart, then it is good I wrote it.

Each one of us has a unique story. My story is no more important than anyone else's. In the tapestry of humanity we all weave together, this book represents a thread of the part I am responsible for. If you are ready, join me on this journey. You may recognize your thread in the tapestry through these adventures!

I share my story to help you understand your stories. To not be afraid of standing in the present moment, not knowing what the future holds. We only have power in the present; the decisions we make today

Introduction | Returning What's Sacred

will affect our tomorrows.

We learn one day at a time, one step at a time, one moment at a time. That is the only way we can know anything, especially during this time of rapid transformation. We need to reconnect with ourselves at this time, and not listen to the outer world so much. It's time to seek our power from within. It is time to know who we are from our soul's perspective and no one else's.

We cannot know what tomorrow will bring or what the world will look like after the changes it is going through. We can only know the present moment.

May my story help bring understanding and peace.

May it bring magic into your life in a way you may not have experienced before; may it inspire you to pay attention to the nuances around you and the hunches you receive from your ancestors and guides.

May you experience trust in the unseen realm, in angels, Spirit and Creator.

And may we all be united as we stand together for the Earth, for humanity, and for peace.

PROLOGUE

White Wolf speaks

"White Wolf is speaking," he announced his presence one day in ceremony, after I had completed the first draft of this book. He channeled the following message:

"The story you've written, the story of the return of the sacred object, is not just your story. It is my story as well. It is the story of what happened to my sacred items. And it needs to be told, not just for you and me, but it needs to be told for all of our People, for our ways have not been respected or honored.

"Our sacred items that carry so much medicine have even been desecrated in these times. It is a way of trying to break us. They don't realize that our sacred objects live inside of us. They don't understand what they're fighting. They don't understand the power that we have. And they don't understand that the power is rising.

"It is coming back to heal our Mother, the Earth, but also to heal our People. For the acknowledgment of what's been done to us, it must happen now. It is time now."

"He could hear his grandfather's words: When one has a purpose in life, one should not worry about anything. For those who keep their purpose in mind, everything will fall into place for them. Today he marveled at his grandfather's wisdom. Everything was happening as if it were planned."

—Violet H. Catches

CHAPTER ONE

MAINE

"Truth-tellers are not popular," my Grandfather has often told me. "It is far easier to point a finger at another when they hold up a mirror to you than it is to face yourself. To face yourself, heal, and grow takes much courage, and many of the human family are not ready to do this."

Grandfather made himself known to me years before I knew who he was, and years before I knew myself to be a truth-teller, or truth-seeker for that matter.

I knew I was different. As a child, I was often content to be alone. Since the age of three, I drew constantly. Once, I made a beaded, fringed dress without any direction—from a place of memory, long before my present life. My mother didn't help me; she couldn't sew a straight line! I saw and knew things I had no reason to as a child.

"Don't tell anyone," my mother would warn, worried that our devoutly Catholic family and friends would brand me as crazy. As a nurse, she had seen people diagnosed and "treated" for such gifts. I learned to keep my visions a closely held secret.

1 | Maine

By my late twenties, I was far along an artistic career path, part of a design team that fed and honored my creativity. I was so happy at the company I worked for, I thought I would never leave. And that might have been the case, had the owner not changed.

A young Harvard businessman brought in to head the business decided to sell it, with no regard for dedicated employees, many of whom lost their jobs. The remaining faced a grueling commute into Boston. Our beautiful, spacious workspace was exchanged for uninspiring cubicles. In hindsight, I see how my soul's purpose was intervening to change the course of my life, but at the time, I felt angry and betrayed, hardly able to keep my feelings in check. After my third(!) car accident on that commute, I knew I had to look elsewhere.

I started to job hunt without a clear direction in mind, so I wasn't getting any replies. One day, after an exceptionally long and traffic-gridlocked drive, I walked into my dark cubby and declared fervently to whoever might be listening:

"I've had it! I want to be where there is ocean and woods!" I finally put words to an intense desire I hadn't named before.

My conviction had such complete and utter emotional strength that as soon as I said it, things aligned to make it happen. I opened a periodical on my desk, and there, before my eyes, popped a job opportunity in Maine for a creative director.

I applied that instant, gathering my samples, putting my resume together, and mailing them. It wasn't more than a couple of days before I got a response. A woman's voice on the phone invited me for an interview. Now that my desire was becoming a reality, I asked, "How far a drive is it from Boston?"

"Five hours," the owner of the design firm, Amina, said firmly. I hesitated a beat.

1 | Maine

"Wow, really? Five hours?" I exclaimed. It hadn't once crossed my mind to think about how far into Maine the job might be!

"How about coming up for the weekend?" Amina responded calmly. "I'll put you up at the bed-and-breakfast in town, and you can come and explore the area." I made plans to come up that weekend and drove to Maine for the first time.

I didn't know about manifestation yet or how the flow of life takes you on a journey. It was the first time in my adult life that I got out of my head and stopped trying to control the outcome. I arrived at the bed and breakfast without event, and decided to go for a ride. As I explored the area, I immediately heard a voice say, "You have the job. You are moving here."

I had never heard anything so crystal clear from the unseen realm. Stunned, I intuitively knew it was true.

This was the first time I heard my Grandfather's voice so distinctly. I did not know yet that he was my Blackfoot grandfather, or anything else about him. Over time, he would stand out as one of my primary, consistent guides from across the veil. I learned to listen for and trust his unerring counsel, even if I'm initially reluctant and occasionally require repetition on his part.

These words, Grandfather didn't need to tell me twice. In less than 24 hours, I accepted the job and planned to move.

Amina found me a cozy little apartment overlooking the ocean, walking distance from the office. This was Amina's way of caring about her people. She had first moved to the area in the 1970s, when she and a group of her friends, disillusioned by the politics in the U.S. at the time, moved to rural Maine. They lived in an old farmhouse, and she and her partner built a teepee during the warmer months. Eventually, they settled, built homes, and became business owners, integrated into

1 | Maine

the fabric of the community.

I felt very excited. Breaking free from all I had ever known and moving to a place where I knew not a soul. It was a courageous fresh start.

What I did not expect was that as soon as I was alone at night in that apartment, my ancestors started talking to me. It was as if, now that I had listened to Grandfather and taken action at his words, the floodgates had opened! Different voices spoke at me, sometimes all at once. I didn't know who they were, but I heard them—not audibly in words, but as fully-formed thoughts coming into my mind. Imagine if your family on the other side suddenly showed up at your bedside at night! It pretty much scared me half to death.

I don't know what let my guard down. Maybe because I didn't know anyone else, maybe because she had already impressed me with her calm, or maybe because I was downright terrified and didn't know what else to do. I went directly to Amina.

I sat down in her office and opened up as if I had known her my entire life. The disconcerting string of events that had occurred since I moved to Maine poured out of me. Scared to tell her about the voices coming to me unbidden in the middle of the night, I told her about the intense dreams I was having instead. And how books that had never interested me before suddenly caught my attention, books about Native culture, a part of my ancestry that I had never really explored. Amina, in her patient way, smiled at me as my torrent of words finally slowed to a trickle. She took a deep breath.

"Native ways happen to be something I have some experience with, and a deep interest in," she said kindly, and without surprise. Ten years my senior, she was more familiar with the synchronicities and flow of life than I was. We had a long conversation about indigenous culture and spirituality.

Gently, Amina guided me out of fear and into curiosity. Thanks to her patient mentorship, I started to surrender to the experience. Over time, I was able to tune in and realize my ancestors were directing me, even suggesting artwork themes and times to paint. When my guides and angels gave me this prayer, word-for-word, I felt complete trust, and knew their guidance came from light and love:

My Creator, My God —
Please guide my spirit through this day—
That I may live my truth, hold my power and integrity.
That I may be thankful for this time of learning,
This incubation period, for my love, my creativity, and myself.
Please help me to be patient, accepting of this time
And to recognize and acknowledge the messages and the gifts
That you constantly send me to sustain my spirit.
Amen, Aho!

Channeling and hearing their direction became a frequent occurrence. I distinctly remember hearing guidance from Grandfather when I started working with stones gathered from nearby beaches. At my artist's table, looking at the stones in my hand, I could feel a slight vibration from some of them and thought that odd. The vibrations ranged from a slow heartbeat to a high, fast pulse. I learned that each frequency corresponded to a different purpose, sometimes for healing, sometimes for grounding energy. Then I heard Grandfather say, "Start playing with them. Put them together."

I started to design jewelry using copper wire to connect the stones, shaping the wire into a spiral to create a pendant. "The spiral

1 | Maine

means to spiral inward toward your path," I heard Spirit say, "toward your true purpose in life and God within."

"The stones ground you to Mother Earth," Spirit continued. "This is the medicine of the pieces that you are creating. These creations will help others on their journey. As you make any piece with these stones, our hands are over your hands. They are being made for someone in particular, and until that person shows up, you will be their keeper. In the end, they will all find who they were made for."

I sat at my art table, astonished. Picking up my journal, I wrote down what I heard verbatim. I no longer felt afraid. I understood that my ancestors were reaching out to me. Maybe they could now reach me because I was in a quiet, solitary environment, contemplating my life in a new way.

Over time, I learned to distinguish between the different voices. Some were my grandmothers, and I started to learn their names. The one who was always there first, though, was Grandfather. I didn't know yet about our shared Blackfoot history. I only knew that we were both "Indian," somehow, some way.

My years in Maine were a magical time for me. When I reflect back, I felt the assistance from the unseen world from the moment I drove into that little town. Native elders would have called me "gifted," as in having spiritual gifts, with an innate artist's sensitivity and deep intuition.

As I was to discover, I was being prepared. Prepared to learn again the wisdom of my ancestors. Prepared to rejoin my family and contemporaries in Ceremony. Step by step, beginning with my experiences in Maine, guided by Grandfather. I share more details about this preparation and remembering who I am in my first book, *Journey of a Red Soul*.

But until I was ready to integrate what my ancestors guided me to remember, I had to be protected. Shielded. Hidden. There was a reason why my ancestry had been hidden from me and why I had been born, not in Canada amongst my people, but in the U.S., to a loving Italian family.

"Who you are is not what you appear to be. This has been your protection. Embrace the blessing of it; do not judge yourself because of outward appearance."

—Grandfather

CHAPTER TWO

MARIE AND ANGELINA

Grandfather said it was critical for my mission this lifetime that I grow up in safety and relative anonymity. (Only later would the reasons why be revealed by Spirit.) He had me born into a close-knit environment as near as he could find to a loving Native family dynamic. This was important because now many mixed-blood people also need healing, including me.

Before my awakening in Maine, I'd been totally immersed in my father's Italian Catholic side of the family. In fact, the more I explored my First Nations heritage, the more my Italian family thought I was going through a "phase."

In reality, I was coming into who I am. As I welcomed my ancestors' guidance, I began putting the pieces together: my ancestors had been calling to me since I was a baby.

Some phase! Since I was born, some phase!

That said, I see how my family's dismissal served my growth, as it only fueled the rebel in me to dive deeper into understanding Native culture.

When I was young, I had no context or support for my gifts. I scared the daylights out of Grammy, my Italian grandmother, who used to take me to church as a baby. I'd see an angel's wing go by and say, "Oh, there's an angel."

Grammy wasn't having any of it! She would shush me, then look at me sideways, with fear in her eyes. I slept over at Grammy's house all the time and would wake up screaming at night. She loved and worried for me. She did not comprehend what was happening to me at all.

Later, as an adult, I would ask, "What's the problem? I don't get it." The first prayer of our church's mass was the Nicene Creed: "We believe in one God, the Father, the Almighty, Maker of all that is, seen and unseen." They're all saying these same words, but scared to death of the unseen realm? I couldn't understand it; it's right in the prayer!

When I started to come out and say, "I hear my Blackfoot grandfather speak to me, and I know when each of my grandmothers are speaking to me," it scared my family even more. Ironically, they had been more comfortable with me seeing angels!

In contrast to my relationships with my father's side of the family, I did not get to know my maternal grandparents, Memé and Pepé, as well. They lived an hour away, so it was a trek to get out there. And as the first grandchild, with my Italian grandparents right in town, it was only natural that I spent much more time with them. (Some would argue that was exactly how Grammy wanted it.)

Memé and Pepé were the ones who linked me to my heritage. I was a child when they passed away. What I remember most about them was the joy, love, and music that flowed when they got together. In their old farm kitchen, my pepé would pull out his banjo while my cousins played their guitars and sang, and my memé beat time with the rocking chair.

What a joy that music created, and what a hole was left when my two favorite uncles died suddenly, before their time. They were quickly followed by Memé. I remember how sad my pepé was that last Christmas after we lost her. Nothing I did could cheer him up and make him his happy self again. We lost him soon after.

Pepé would proudly say, "We are Algonquin," not knowing that Algonquin is the dialect and that we are Wolastoqiyik (Maliseet). But Memé would never even admit to being Blackfoot and Mi'kmaq because, in her experience, you didn't tell people that you were "Indian." It was looked down upon. Natives were called *sauvages*, from Latin roots meaning of the wood or forest (*silvan*) and wild (*salvus*). Later, the "u" was dropped and the word became a pejorative, "savage."

Memé's secrecy was a survival mechanism. She had been taught that to be safe, you had to erase who you were. And she was angry; she thought her "Indian" mother had abandoned her.

Memé had been thrown into an orphanage when her mother died. I share her story in *Journey of a Red Soul*:

> "We were always told that my memé's mother had taken her own life. Her three children were all thrown into an orphanage afterward by their father… Memé's older brother was able to leave the orphanage after a few years because of his age. Her younger sister was adopted and had a decent life. But my memé was not so lucky. She was shuffled from foster home to foster home until she was old enough to get out of the system. I've only heard stories of a few of the horrible things she endured. She always felt that her mother had abandoned her, but this was not the reality…
>
> "We got on the topic of our Native lineage because I was doing research into our genealogy at the time. My mom had recently received some photos of my great-grandmother and other family mem-

bers, and we started looking through them. We began discussing the story we had always been told, of how my memé had been put into the orphanage after her mother's suicide. Moments later, I left my mom and walked down the hallway to retrieve something from the bedroom when I suddenly heard the following in a shockingly forceful and angry tone. I knew immediately it was my great-grandmother.

"I DID NOT COMMIT SUICIDE! I would NEVER have left my children to that monster!"

"He murdered me because I was Native and strong-willed!" I heard her continue. I knew she must mean her husband, who was French-Canadian. "He poisoned me right in front of my children! I would never have abandoned my children to that monster! You tell the family the truth!"

Stunned, I relayed my great-grandmother's words to my mom. It was time to clear her name. I proceeded to tell my mother's sisters and some cousins, those surviving family members who were ready to hear the truth.

My great-grandfather was not aware that Angelina was Native when he married her. Angelina's family was able to "pass" as (white) French Canadians because Northeast Woodland First Nations people tend to have lighter skin. So, unless they had distinct facial features, you could not necessarily tell by skin tone alone. Also, since Marie lived in Matane on the Gaspé peninsula, it was a more populated area, near but not on a reservation. This also helped her hide her heritage. Her mother, Louise, born in northern Saskatchewan, deep in "Indian country," would not have had that privilege.

Once my great-grandfather realized that Angelina was Native, he wanted nothing to do with her or his own children.

Angelina's mother, Marie, had made the decision to hide their ancestry when her children were young. I didn't fully understand her reasons why until years later, when she appeared to me as powerful and commanding as Angelina had been.

I was getting ready to put out my first book, and my publisher wanted me to come up with a pen name. I resisted at first and struggled to choose a name. I took some time off and went to spend a few days with my parents.

"I don't understand why I have to come up with a pen name in the first place," I said in frustration. The identities of all of the people involved had been made anonymous. It felt like the publishing house's concern went above and beyond protecting the people involved (and their liability), as if they were threatened by the metaphysical nature of the experiences I wrote about.

My mom woke up the next morning with the answer. "I know what name you should use," she said, with a glimmer in her eye. My mom gets her insights and clarity at night. She doesn't remember the dreams; she just comes out of them with a clear answer.

"Really?" I said. "What is it?"

"I woke up knowing," she said matter-of-factly. "Your great-great grandmother's name, Marie Dion!"

I walked out on the deck to ponder my mom's message. There, I had a vision of my great-great-grandmother, Marie, Angelina's mother, walking into a kitchen. She slammed her fist on the counter.

"Use my name," she demanded, in no uncertain terms. "So I can protect you and claim who I AM."

Marie continued, "First, I can protect you from some unforeseen things, including people's judgments for sharing your truth."

"Second, when I was alive, they were taking all the Native children from their families and putting them in residential schools!" she said vehemently. "I had to deny my culture and pretend I was French so I didn't lose my children."

Marie asked me to clear her name, just as Angelina did before her. Both had been judged without understanding the true circumstances of their situation and time.

Marie lived during the mid-1800s. There was such pervasive fear at that time. Government agents just took the children away! "Kill the Indian in him, and save the man," General Richard Henry Pratt's words became the residential schools' motto, forbidding students from speaking their language or carrying out any of their traditional practices and training them instead to be servants.[1] Marie wanted me to use her name so that she could clear the karma of denying her culture—and begin to heal the lineage of all the mothers who lost their children to the schools.

It was then that I understood why and how my Native ancestry had been downplayed, hidden, and denied. Many who experienced the residential schools were deeply traumatized—if they survived!

Not long after Marie demanded that I use her name, residential schools began to be covered more widely in the media. Marie's fear was valid; parents never saw their kids again, in most cases. Stories all over the news covered graves found at residential school sites in the U.S. and Canada.[2]

The influence of my ancestors in my life connected me with this unknown side of my family once more. Grandfather and others guided me to places, gatherings, and locations that had some significance or meaning to my history so I could painstakingly piece the details together.

I found myself at powwows or invited to ceremonies, all of which seemed guided and synchronistic. My ancestors showed me a little at a time as I was ready to receive the information: what it meant to be a mixed-blood. I would come to be very proud of the part of my lineage that had been hidden away, covered up, shunned, and marginalized by a culture that did not understand us. Every day in that Maine town, I reconnected and healed my lineage. I painted our memories—all unconsciously at the time, of course, but I sensed that this path was my destiny.

When I came home to visit, my Italian family's shock at who I had become, especially my sisters' dismay, was hard to take. Most had no idea about my spiritual gifts; only my mother knew about the dreams, nightmares, and visions I'd struggled with my entire life.

No one understood that my identity had shifted on a fundamental level. I was finding myself and the answers I'd sought before I knew the questions. My understanding of spiritual teachings grew, an understanding I'd yearned for that had eluded me until then. It was as if my ancestors took over. It was time for me to know who I was, and they were going to show me, with Grandfather at the helm.

---

[1] "US Indian Boarding School History." The National Native American Boarding School Healing Coalition, ~2020, boardingschoolhealing.org/education/us-indian-boarding-school-history/.

[2] Sources include:
"Canada: 751 Unmarked Graves Found at Residential School." BBC, 24 Jun. 2021, www.bbc.com/news/world-us-canada-57592243.

Lindeman, Tracey. "Canada: Remains of 215 Children Found at Indigenous Residential School Site." The Guardian, 28 May 2021, www.theguardian.com/world/2021/may/28/canada-remains-indigenous-children-mass-graves.

Hopkins, Ruth. "Unmarked Graves at Indian Residential Schools Speak to Horrors Faced By Students." Teen Vogue, 14 Jul. 2021, www.teenvogue.com/story/indian-residential-schools-graves.

The Associated Press. "U.S. Report Identifies Burial Sites Linked to Boarding Schools for Native Americans." National Public Radio, 11 May 2022, www.npr.org/2022/05/11/1098276649/u-s-report-details-burial-sites-linked-to-boarding-schools-for-native-americans.

"I see a time of Seven Generations when all the colors of mankind will gather under the Sacred Tree of Life and the whole Earth will become One Circle again."

—Crazy Horse

CHAPTER THREE

SEVEN GENERATIONS

I want to thank my great-great-grandmother Marie Dion, whose name I carry as an author, for saving her children from the residential school system at the expense of denying her culture. The more I learn about that time, the more I understand how brave she was. My hope in carrying her name and acknowledging our culture is that it creates a ripple effect that heals the pain of that loss—the loss of culture and our indigenous extended family.

Thank you, Grandmother Marie, for having the courage to risk everything to save your children. For I am here now because of you. Because your children survived. I walk the Red Road now because of you and my Blackfoot grandfather. I am here because of your prayers. I am here because of your faith. I come from such an amazing line of strong, faithful people, and I am truly humbled and proud to walk this path.

Healing what has happened to our people is why I am here, living in this time. Grandmother, walk beside me as I go forward on this path; give me your strength and courage to be a part of the healing.

While living in Maine, I dreamt that I heard my ancestors calling

3 | Seven generations

my spirit name over and over as I rode through crowds of First Nations people. They had hope in their eyes as they said my name. They had hope in their voices as they repeated it.

Grandfather revealed his name, "Onachowa. It means 'the one who speaks with Spirit.' Your spirit name means the same."

"You are the point of the arrow to pierce through the other dimensions, other worlds," he continued. "You'll see these in your waking time. This is a great gift you've been given. The arrowhead is the first to pierce through the darkness."

Grandfather told me often, "I did big, big ceremonies so that you would remember. As the seventh-generation grandchild." That I would be born knowing, and uncover the memories, putting the pieces together as I was ready to understand.

"Our people were told what was to come," he said. "We were told to be prepared. Our families would forget all the ways of our people for many generations. But if our ceremonies were strong, the seventh generation would remember. You would remember and bring back these ways."

Grandfather's words were repeated by an Elder named Billie, whom I met in Lakota country in 2019.

"This is the prophecy, the warning that the Spirits had given the people before the Europeans came to this continent," Billie said. "Seven generations would pass before our ways would be remembered and practiced."

"The people were guided to make big ceremonies for the future seventh generation, gathering medicines and power," he continued. "And over the course of those seven generations, an unraveling of the ways would happen. The people would lose their deep connection to the Earth and the ways of their ancestors."

3 | Seven generations

"Then the seventh generation would arrive. Become curious. And have a desire to get back to the traditions and search for what was lost. They would reestablish the balance and bring the ways back to the people and heal the Earth."

"The prophecy was clear: every generation would lose more of their connection to their culture until the seventh generation arrived and returned. This is why the ceremonies had to be done before the continent was invaded. Before the energy of the Europeans came."

> "From my memories of my past lives, I recall these words that were said by the elders to the white soldiers who were involved in the massacres during the westward expansion:
>
> 'We will be born again and return as your sons and daughters.'
>
> From what I have been told by my ancestors, this has come to pass as a way to help create the needed empathy between the souls that have had either a European or Native history."—from *Journey of a Red Soul*

As guides like Grandfather would reveal to me, despite my outward appearance and upbringing, I was a red soul reborn in a white body, just as our ancestors predicted seven generations ago, with the additional gift of a bloodline still connected to my Native lineage. My mixed blood allows me to traverse dangerous waters, mostly undetected, so I can help my people.

I am the seventh generation that my grandfather prayed for. He prayed our ways would not be forgotten and that his children's children, to seven generations, would one day remember who they are.

I pray to be a voice for those who have been forgotten.

I pray for the healing of the grandmothers and grandfathers, fathers and mothers who came before me, as well as for the seven generations yet to come.

3 | Seven generations

It is time to heal history and create something beautiful. The healing needs to happen for my people, for all peoples, so that we create a new world where "human" is the only definition of race.

This is the world that we can create for ourselves and our future.

As a seventh-generation descendant, I can only do my best to fulfill that which is asked of me. I can only walk this path moment by moment. Right here, right now. Every choice I make creates my next step on the journey.

I had no idea how true that was going to become… or how the next step would appear in the most unlikely of places.

3 | Seven generations

"When you're selected by the spirit world, there's a reason. You feel obligated and privileged that they call on you. I feel a sense of duty to get this done. I would like the spirits to say, You did what we wanted you to do; you were committed."

—Clifford Canku

CHAPTER FOUR

A GUN SHOW IN MASSACHUSETTS

Early in my relationship with my husband-to-be, Damon, he wanted to visit a gun show in our local area. He asked me and another friend to join him. I had never been to one, so I was curious.

I don't take the purchase of guns lightly. Damon and I hunt and raise our own food, though, so that includes having the proper equipment. I don't take hunting lightly either: my belief is that, when we hunt, we must honor the animals that we take. I pray before we leave, asking the spirit of the animal to come to us, for we are in need of food. When an animal offers itself to you after such prayers have been said, it is of the highest respect to take the gift that is given. That energy of respect and honor goes into the meat.

When we walked into the gun show, right in front, I saw a non-Native vendor selling Native items. Immediately suspicious, I made a beeline toward him. The first item that caught my eye was a sacred object for sale on his table…! It was a pipe, its protective wraps removed, fully assembled, and ready for ceremony!

"What are you doing with this?!" I gasped, overwhelmed with

rage at the disrespect.

Sacred objects are never to be touched by anyone other than their owner without permission, let alone used or sold. I was shocked and furious all at once. I could see that the pipe was very old and had eagle feathers attached to it. My ancestors informed me it was stolen from a grave out west.

"How did you get it? Why do you have it put together as if it's ready for use in ceremony?" I demanded.

Nervous, the seller refused to name his source. I could barely breathe; the words rushed out of me in fury. "How dare you disrespect my people! This is a sacred pipe and is not allowed to be sold. These are eagle feathers! You know, these are illegal for a non-Native to own." It could mean jail time and thousands of dollars in fines if he were caught with them.[3]

"I'm going to get that police officer over there and have you arrested," I turned toward the officer on duty.

"Whoa, wait a minute..." The vendor waved his hands, panicked. "Hold on, let's talk about this." Totally flustered, he quickly took the pipe apart and hid it under his table.

"How did it come into your possession?" I asked.

He dodged my question again and, instead, tried to distract me with questions about who I was and how I knew about these things. I was not deterred. "I am not leaving without that pipe! And you're not allowed to sell it."

"Well, what will you give me for it?" he started to bargain.

"A sacred object cannot be bought or sold," I reiterated angrily. "I know you have it illegally. It's very old. It can't be purchased!"

"Well, I'm not going to just give it to you," he said warily, crossing his arms over his chest.

We were at a standstill. I was about to get the policeman when the friend that was with us chimed in, "She's an amazing artist. Why don't you trade her for it?" She had been behind him, eyes wide, throughout the verbal confrontation.

He looked at me, startled. "Is that true?"

"Yes," I nodded, surprised we could come to terms. "I'll trade you for it." We proceeded to make arrangements. I would return with my artwork the next day before the show opened. He would meet me around back in the parking lot. We would trade, and in exchange, I would not report him to the police.

Early the next morning, when Damon and I got in his truck to meet the vendor, a vision consumed me as I slid into the passenger seat. Suddenly, I was flanked by long rows of warriors to my right and left. More than 20 lined up on each side of me on horseback! They were as angry as I was.

They were not my ancestors, but warriors from the tribe associated with the pipe. They looked at me, letting me know that I was not going alone. They were with me and ready for battle. I thought to myself, *He had better give this pipe to me, or he is in big trouble!*

We arrived. The vendor was there waiting. I had filled the back of the truck with my artwork, original sculptures, rugs, and jewelry, not knowing which he would prefer. I figured he would pick a few of the pieces. Greedily, he demanded everything I brought before he would hand over the pipe. I did not care.

The vendor was sly. He held up the beaded bag he had with the pipe and asked arrogantly, "What will you give me for this?"

"You can keep the bag," I dismissed him, dumbfounded. He really didn't get the gravity of the situation. "It doesn't go with the pipe anyway." The bag, though beautiful, was too new to have belonged

4 | A gun show in Massachusetts

with the object.

Spirit was clear, *Take it and go*. My guides wanted me out of his presence as soon as possible.

Damon and I left. A wave of relief washed over me. I felt as if I had saved a baby, it was that precious. The unseen warriors escorted us all the way home in gratitude.

---

[3] "You can't take or even move any part of a bald eagle, not even a feather already on the ground. A single violation could result in up to one year in prison and a $5,000 fine."

Coble, Christopher Esq. "If I Find an Eagle Feather, Can I Keep It?" Find Law, 21 Mar. 2019, www.findlaw.com/legalblogs/law-and-life/if-i-find-an-eagle-feather-can-i-keep-it/.

4 | A gun show in Massachusetts

"Take the first step in faith. You don't have to see the whole staircase, just take the first step."

—Martin Luther King Jr.

CHAPTER FIVE

NOW WHAT?

When I got home, I looked the sacred object over tenderly as I smudged it with sage and wrapped each piece in red cloth. I brought the wrapped bundle into my medicine wheel to pray over it for direction, innately knowing not to use it. I wondered about its story and what should be done. Going back inside, I felt a big sense of relief as I placed the bundle on my altar.

Within days, I received an invitation to go to a sweat lodge two weeks later. A Lakota man, Nick, would be conducting and pouring the sweat. I'd known him and his family for many years as a fellow vendor and watched his daughter grow up at the cultural craft fairs we did together.

Nick will know what to do with the sacred object, I thought to myself. *Maybe I can give it to him? He will know how to take care of it properly.* I took it with me when I went to attend the lodge.

We sat together prior to going into the ceremony, and I told him the story of how I acquired the pipe. I asked him to pray with me about it. He said he would, and see if we got any messages from Spirit. "Let's

5 | Now what?

talk again after the sweat," he concluded.

I have regularly attended traditional sweat lodge ceremonies for many years, but had never been to a Lakota sweat lodge. The sweat lodges are run slightly differently according to traditions.

"I got a clear message," Nick said, after we finished the ceremony.

"Ok, let's hear it," I replied.

"You have to take it back to the Black Hills, in South Dakota, to put it to rest." The Black Hills are within treaty territory, recognized by the U.S. as part of the reservation for exclusive use by the People of the Seven Council Fires (Oceti Sakowin Oyate, pronounced o-chay-tee / shah-go-weehn/nasal vowel / oy-yah-tay).[4] They were never for sale; they were never sold. They are sacred.

"I HAVE TO DO WHAT?!" I exclaimed. Because of our long relationship, I didn't edit myself. The look on his face read total shock at my response. It wasn't that I didn't respect what he had to tell me, but it was so far from any concept of what I thought needed to be done that I couldn't get my head around it.

I did not react to the message well, verbally attacking the messenger. "I've never been out there. I don't know where to go!" I yelled. I just wanted him to take the pipe off my hands! I thought I had already done my job in saving it.

That was not Spirit's wish, however. The sacred pipe was now my responsibility.

"How am I supposed to do that?" I continued. "My people are from the Eastern woodlands, I don't know Western ways! I don't know where to go!"

He responded calmly and matter-of-factly. "You just fly out, rent a car and drive to where they do ceremony in the Black Hills. And put it to rest."

"No worries," he added, seeing that his words had little effect to calm me. "You have ten years to do it."

As it would happen, that was the last time I saw Nick. The journey with the sacred object was mine, and it had just begun.

---

[4] Sioux Native Americans: Their History, Culture, and Traditions. (2021, August 1). Native Hope. April 21, 2024, https://blog.nativehope.org/sioux-native-americans-their-history-culture-and-traditions

"Never be afraid to raise your voice for honesty and truth
and compassion against injustice and lying and greed.
If people all over the world...would do this,
it would change the Earth."

—William Faulkner

CHAPTER SIX

THE PIPE'S STORY, REVEALED

I was daunted by the task ahead of me, but relieved that I had time to figure it out. Little did I know that it would take every one of those ten years to prepare the pipe—and me!—to return it to its final place of rest.

I sensed that because of the sacredness of this pipe, it needed healing from the trauma it had been through before it could be put to rest. I felt that it had carried many prayers in its time, and now needed some of its own. Although I didn't yet know its history, it had clearly been greatly disrespected to end up on a vendor's table at a gun show in Massachusetts, far from its home in the Black Hills. I knew enough to know that it had been taken by a thief with no regard for my people.

As I wrote this, White Wolf, the pipe's owner, whom I would get to know well, began to explain. "The story of me surviving the buffalo hunt traveled far." I would hear more of this legend later from my Blackfoot chief.

"My prowess in battle had earned me many accolades," White Wolf continued, "The thief was not a warrior but a scavenger. He was

6 | The pipe's story, revealed

a soldier in the same regiment as the man who killed me, but he didn't have courage. He wasn't even in the battle; he was part of the clean-up crew after."

"The soldier wanted to brag that he had killed such a powerful Native warrior, even though he hadn't," he said. He just needed "proof" to corroborate the story.

When I later traveled to South Dakota, I learned that White Wolf was Cheyenne. The Cheyenne, like many other tribes, honor their deceased with family and tribal members by keeping vigil over them, surrounded by their personal belongings, for four days before burying them.[5]

"When my things were still above ground before I was buried, the scavenger stumbled upon us. This is when he saw my pipe and got fixated on it." White Wolf continued. "I see him hidden, lying on the ground, watching while my people were distracted in their grief."

"The thief came back in the night after my people had buried my body and left the area. He dug up the fresh grave and took many of my things."

The Cheyenne were not afraid of the unseen world and its natural processes because they respected and understood it. Their burial practices were built around the soul's journey to the other side. By contrast, in fear and ignorance of the unseen world and what they don't understand, soldiers unknowingly disrupted those natural processes when they disturbed a burial site, wreaking havoc and creating unrest in the world of Spirit.

Later, it was revealed to me that White Wolf's sacred pipe was hidden in a box for many years after it was stolen, stored away in a descendant's attic. What was once a prized memento for the scavenger became a source of shame for his family. The resonance of the injustice rippled to his descendants, who just wanted the object out of the house.

The trespass of sacred burial sites stirs up the unseen world, causing a rift in the harmony between the physical realm and the realm of Spirit. The wounding doesn't just happen for those whose graves are disturbed; it also happens for those who disturb them, scarring land, items, and people for generations to come.

And that is how a sacred object, stolen from the Black Hills of South Dakota, came to travel, change hands, and be on the market for sale—eventually finding its way to a gun show in Massachusetts.

---

[5] KMKennedy164. "The Funeral Practices of the Blackfoot and Cheyenne Tribes." *West of the Frontier: Death and Dying on the Great Plains,* 11 Feb. 2015, westofthefrontierdeathanddying.wordpress.com/2015/02/11/the-funeral-practices-of-the-blackfoot-and-cheyenne-tribes/.

"I can control my destiny, but not my fate. Destiny means there are opportunities to turn right or left, but fate is a one-way street. I believe we all have the choice as to whether we fulfill our destiny, but our fate is sealed."

—Paulo Coelho

CHAPTER SEVEN

THE PIPE'S HEALING

My interaction with Nick was only a month before I was to go to Canada that fall. Not much liking the answer he had given me, I decided I would take the sacred object with me and see my Mi'kmaq chief, Wayne. Also, I had no idea what exactly it was that I had ten years to do. I would ask my chief to pray about it so we could figure out the next proper step.

I trusted that Wayne would know what to do with a pipe because he took care of all the pipes in our Ceremony. And I knew he was connected enough that he would get the right message. Wayne instructed me before I left, "When you come up, just bring the pipe and leave the remaining bundle on the altar."

After I arrived and shared the story with my Mi'kmaq chief and his wife, she reprimanded me. "You don't ask one medicine person what to do and then not like the answer and go to another one," she said. "You don't do that." She was right, and I nodded my agreement, humbly taking her words to heart. She always was a voice of reason.

Wayne had one of the women summon me in the middle of the

7 | The pipe's healing

night when he got the answer of what needed to be done. "The pipe has been part of the ceremonies that we conduct," he explained.

Then I heard Grandfather say, "It is for this reason that the warriors showed up and flanked you when you went to retrieve it."

"The pipe needs to go through four years of ceremonies to heal," Wayne continued.

Four years passed quickly. Over the ten years from the day I found the sacred object to the day I left to return it to its final resting place, I ran a gauntlet of experiences and challenges that I later realized were required preparations for the journey.

7 | The pipe's healing

"Faith is the strength by which a shattered world shall emerge into the light."

—Helen Keller

CHAPTER EIGHT

ON THE HOMEFRONT

You may be wondering how all this was sitting with my then-fiancé, Damon. A self-proclaimed "Swamp Yankee," he'd spent most of his life working his family's homestead farm.[6] "Countrified, stubborn, and independent?" That's Damon. You just don't get much more salt-of-the-earth than him

Before we started dating, I asked him flat out. "Okay, you want a date with me? How do you feel about spirits?"

I'd been on my path long enough to know that anyone who wanted to be with me was going to have to be comfortable with the whole package. And by that point in my life, I honestly didn't believe that men could handle my gifts. I figured that if I just told Damon about them, he would run for the hills.

"Oh, they're real! I've seen them!" Damon replied, stunning me. He eagerly started sharing his stories. "Once, when I was younger, I was babysitting and saw an orb of light go down a hallway. There was no explanation for it!"

"And after my mother died, I cleaned out the kitchen... In the middle of the night, bam, bam, bam-BAM! All the kitchen cabinet doors slammed shut more than once. It scared the shit out of me and my dog! She was mad!! I knew it had to be my mom, pissed with me for throwing out all her Tupperware. I threw out a couple truckloads!"

"Really?!" was all I managed to get out in my surprise. I felt encouraged that he was open, but still wondered how he'd react. I wasn't even sure I wanted a relationship and was as much trying to deflect Damon's interest as scope him out.

"What if I told you I can hear spirits and speak to them?" I tested him.

"I'd believe you," he said matter-of-factly. I gave in at that point and agreed to a first date. I would later learn that his great-aunt was a world-renowned medium. She used to create drawings with personal messages from Spirit in the middle of the dining room of the home where we now live! Believing was in his lineage.

As much as that was true, it was still a challenge for him to wholeheartedly trust in guidance from Spirit the way I had learned to. That challenge came to a head when we ended up having a heated discussion about our future.

It was January of 2015, seven years after we started dating and six years since White Wolf's sacred pipe had been entrusted to me. We had been living together for years and were engaged to be married.

I don't remember all the details of the argument, just that I was getting information about our future, and Damon was having a hard time understanding me or my confidence in what I was receiving.

"You need to trust the unseen world," I argued. He grunted, waving his hand dismissively, and stayed put on the couch, turning his attention back to the TV.

Frustrated and at a loss, it was a poignant crossroads for me. *How*

8 | On the homefront

could we stay together if he doesn't take my guidance seriously? I thought. Not that Damon doesn't believe in my gifts; he does, and has seen my foresight play out—but always with a sense of surprise.

A straightforward guy, he is wary of putting stock in just about anything. When he was a younger man, he got into a serious motorcycle accident the week before he was to fix trucks for the Army in Vietnam. As someone whose life's plan totally flipped with that one event, you could see how he might put little faith in anyone's future vision, or the idea that our prayers can not only be heard but answered.

His doubt, though, felt like he didn't trust me, which hurt deeply. Often, in the past, I had requested a sign and received it, usually in the form of a feather with a distinct message. This time, I wanted proof that even Damon couldn't deny.

"Help me find a 'shed' so that I can prove to him that you hear me," I asked the spirits.

It was around the time of year when the deer start shedding their antlers, or "sheds" for short. Elsewhere in the area, you could easily find them around, but in all the time I'd known Damon, we'd only ever found one shed on the farm. "I need to prove to him that you hear me," I prayed fervently.

After sending up this request, I searched and searched the fields but found nothing. I looked for about an hour and then went into my wheel to pray. I took another look around as I left, but still, nothing. Surprised and disappointed, I thought, *There isn't going to be proof…*

In that moment, I saw it, a shed in the very first place I had looked: near a feeder for the critters we had in the back field. There had been nothing there before. Now, as I walked back past it, there was a fresh shed, still wet with blood. A young buck must have appeared and rubbed it off while I prayed in the medicine wheel.

8 | On the homefront

They heard me, I thought. I knew it with total and utter confidence. Now I could show the antler to Damon, and dispel his doubt—or at least, for the time being. More importantly, I felt heard and validated by Spirit. This wasn't just about Damon; it was about solidifying my own faith.

---

[6] "Swamp Yankee is a colloquial term for rural New Englanders who are mainly of colonial English descent and Protestant background. The term "Yankee" carries connotations of urbane industriousness and the Protestant work ethic, while "Swamp Yankee" suggests a more countrified, stubborn, independent, and less-refined sub-type."

From "Swamp Yankee." *Wikipedia,* Wikimedia Foundation, 30 May 2023, en.wikipedia.org/wiki/Swamp_Yankee.

8 | On the homefront

"I have seen that in any great undertaking it is not enough for a man to depend simply upon himself."

—Teton proverb

CHAPTER NINE

MEETING WHITE WOLF

Four years into this odyssey, when I received the sacred pipe back from its healing journey in our ceremonies, the spirit that it belonged to introduced himself to me. (You've already met him in the course of this book.)

In truth, he started letting himself be known to me from the moment I rescued the pipe; I just didn't yet know his name. I could see him and feel his good heart.

It wasn't long before I brought the pipe into the wheel to pray, accompanied by my cousin Wyn. It was there that its owner spoke to us, addressing me directly.

"My name is White Wolf," he said. "I no longer have any living relatives for the pipe to go to. That is why it needs to be put to rest now, since all my relatives are gone."

"I am a brother to you through our ceremonies," he said to me, confirming the message my Mi'kmaq chief had received about the sacred object.

White Wolf expressed his shock at my life. "I feel sorry for you," he said. "As I watch you having to do women's things *and* men's things in life—and at such a fast pace! In my time, the women did not participate in ceremonies as they do now; it was only the men. The women's and men's roles were very separate and balanced."

I was humbled one afternoon when he said, "You impress me. I want to help you in your life. I am grateful for all you have done for me."

White Wolf helped orchestrate circumstances in ways I couldn't even begin to imagine, from helping me to see the true nature of a toxic client relationship to arranging for me to heal and reclaim a very piece of my soul.

"You earned the help," he is saying as I write these words. "Through your selflessness and your willingness to take on a task that seemed insurmountable to you."

Sooner than later, I would call on that help when the events at Standing Rock shifted my reality.

9 | Meeting White Wolf

"In the history of colonization, they've always given us two options: Give up our land or go to jail. Give up our rights or go to jail. And now, give up our water or go to jail."

—Woman of the Standing Rock Sioux

CHAPTER TEN

THE BEAR AWAKENS

In 2016, hundreds of people gathered to join the Standing Rock Sioux's peaceful protest of the construction of the Dakota Access Pipeline (DAPL), an oil pipeline that would stretch across the Dakotas and Iowa to Illinois, desecrating land and potentially contaminating drinking water for thousands on the Standing Rock reservation and millions downstream.[7]

It is a desecration because, as Ava, a Hohwoju Lakota elder from the Cheyenne River Reservation and third-generation Oglala Sioux descendant who you'll meet later, reminded me, "sacred and land are synonymous, not separate. We are the Sioux who fight the black snake. Others joined us in our fight for our sacred grandmother, the earth and what she provides for us."

Standing Rock was the fulfillment of a centuries-old Oceti Sakowin prophecy of the black snake. They were told that if it wasn't stopped, the black snake would bring destruction and hardship to the land and people. It seemed evident that DAPL and other pipelines like it were the black snake.

10 | The bear awakens

My social media started to blow up. I saw the youth raising awareness and felt proud.[8] But as things escalated, images of private guards threatening protesters with dogs shocked me.[9] *What?! What is happening?* I thought.

I couldn't believe that the persecution of Native peoples was happening again, and I was watching it, live. It seemed like history repeating itself. I couldn't get any work done, I felt so activated and angry.

Then LaDonna Brave Bull Allard posted a video with the appeal, "Please come and stand with us."[10]

This is how Standing Rock burst into my awareness.

And I wasn't alone. All of a sudden, it seemed like every Native on the continent woke up. Everybody came together! It was the first time I had seen so many indigenous people gathered, from all over the world. It was historic, a coming together of tribes like never before.

Standing Rock consumed my life. Every day, I watched livestreams from people on the ground and hung on to every update. Outside Indian country, the protest was largely invisible, barely reported in mainstream media. Many people, even today, have no idea what happened at Standing Rock.

It was such an important time for us to support each other. People joined the protest in waves, some showing up with nothing. The water protectors needed everything, including coats, as the protest stretched into the brutal Dakota winter. Feeding everyone became the biggest concern. My friend May, whose sons were already at Standing Rock, was collecting funds and supplies to take with her from Maine to South Dakota. We connected so I could help spread the word.

I watched in horror as my people were attacked as they stood in peaceful protest on their own land. My brothers and sisters constantly shared all of this, live, on social media, in videos that the platform later

10 | The bear awakens

took down:

Water cannons pummeled them in the freezing temperatures. Rubber bullets pierced skin, some causing devastating injuries. Protesters were regularly sprayed in the face with mace. They washed their eyes at multiple stations and headed right back into the fray. May told me that helicopters flew low and loud over the camps night after night so that no one could sleep. Their experience was the very definition of psychological torture.

The water protectors asked us to share photos of the escalating violence so that we could educate people about what was happening at Standing Rock. That's when I understood how fragmented our country is, and how corrupt. Again, Native lives were nothing more than collateral damage in the way of what these companies wanted. And still want: the pipeline remains in operation as litigation and challenges continue.[11]

It's as if we're eating ourselves from the inside out, totally destroying ourselves by destroying our environment. Or being complacent and allowing greed to destroy our environment and each other.

At the time, I was desperately trying to figure out how to get to Standing Rock. Except: Grandfather insisted, "NO! You cannot go out there now!"

I fought him hard. I felt that standing with my people at this historic moment was why I was born. I argued, and pleaded, and prayed, and railed against him. And, I also trusted there must be a reason why Grandfather was dead set against my going. I relented and resigned myself to doing everything else in my power to help.

So I did a lot of prayers in my medicine wheel. I did a lot of raising money. I was literally on social media every single day, posting, educating, sending stuff everywhere, connecting people, and protesting locally.

I tried to educate the predominantly white area that I live in on what was occurring at Standing Rock. I created and printed a 17-foot banner with images taken directly from the front lines. I hung it across the front of my barn so it faced a main road. At night, I focused blue lights that rippled like moving water across the banner.

The only people who seemed to notice were already in full support. A woman who was fighting a local pipeline saw the banner at night. She excitedly pulled up when she saw me outside so she could take pictures with me in front of it.

Damon and I attended an event at the VFW. I asked the emcee if I could speak to the crowd and tell them about what was happening out west. My words were met with silence, which, in hindsight, I could have predicted. I sensed that Standing Rock was so far outside of their awareness that they couldn't hear me. I felt frustrated and powerless.

That summer, my activist friend Kate planned to head out to the protest. Before she left, we prayed together in preparation. I gave her something sacred to bring there, so I could connect and put my prayers on the land in a respectful, quiet way.

Kate was there a couple of weeks before she found a spot that felt right, behind a teepee. As she finished, she looked up to see two horses run from far across the camp to graze at the exact spot where she had just performed this prayer for me. She took this as a sign that the prayers were heard and accepted by the spirits.

People on the East Coast gathered everywhere in solidarity with Standing Rock. A protest was arranged in northern Maine, to happen that November—in the middle of a busy intersection on Black Friday! May, back from the Dakotas, invited me to join them. Her sons remained at the camps. We unexpectedly ended up in not one but two full-color photos on the front cover of the local newspaper: in one, I hugged May as I emotionally welcomed her back from Standing Rock, and in the other, my sisters and brothers and I drummed in protest.[12]

One by one, the camps fell until there was only one of the original three left.[13] The police came in and ripped my relatives' tents apart, putting everything in a big pile and setting it ablaze. Shocked, I posted:

"Our Relatives were pulled out of prayer and the sweat lodge while in ceremony!!!! AND Arrested for trying to protect sacred items which are being taken by police!!!! Why? They are not weapons???? Our religious rights are NOT being honored! Is this the 1700s? 1800s?? NO, it's 2016!!!! Relatives, I honor your courage, and I pray for you in every moment and with every breath I take."

As intensely as I wanted to join them in person, Grandfather never allowed me to go out to Standing Rock. "You would become too traumatized," he said. "You would not be able to fulfill your purpose if you went out and participated in Standing Rock." It was not yet time for me to go to South Dakota.

I would see Grandfather's words borne out in the people who participated on the front lines of the protest. It truly was a modern-day battleground. Many were arrested. Others are still dealing with court cases. The PTSD that protesters suffer to this day is real—especially since all the sacrifices they made and the pain they endured didn't succeed in stopping the pipeline.

I also saw how traumatized I felt just witnessing the events at Standing Rock from afar. We were so hopeful when the protest started that we would be the ones to stop the black snake. And then, so deflated, disenfranchised, and heartbroken after, when the brutality we met went unpunished and unacknowledged, once again.

Damon, seeing me so distraught, took me to our favorite Chinese restaurant in our weekly Friday night ritual. I could barely lift my head to eat, I felt so defeated. Finally, the fortune cookies came, and I half-heartedly cracked one open. The message was so timely and comforting in that moment, I saved it so I can pull it out and look at it whenever I need to:

"Spirit guides accompany you."

"There was a reason you could not go to Standing Rock," White Wolf is saying as I write this. "Here is where history was repeating itself. This was one of your life's potential pitfalls that you needed to be protected from until you were ready. Ready in spirit and full understanding to walk forward and fulfill the mission ahead of you."

So instead… I wrote a book. At the height of these events, my ancestors started waking me in the mornings to channel. In these early morning recordings, the ancestors spoke through me the words that would become my first book, *Journey of a Red Soul*. It seemed like a way to funnel the tremendous emotions that ran through me nonstop during that time.

Standing Rock changed me forever. It incited me to take action in a way that was completely out of character for me. As someone who was much more comfortable supporting behind the scenes, that time saw me proclaiming who I was and what I stood for in a very public way. The experience prepared me in ways I couldn't even imagine for the next steps on my journey, and as the (temporary) custodian of White Wolf's sacred pipe.

Standing Rock woke a sleeping bear in me.

⁷ There is so much more to say about Standing Rock that is beyond the scope of this book. I encourage you to learn more about what happened in the Resources section and in your own research.

⁸ Petronzio, Matt. "How Young Native Americans Built and Sustained the #NoDAPL Movement." *Mashable,* 7 Dec. 2016, mashable.com/article/standing-rock-nodapl-youth.

⁹ "Guards Accused of Unleashing Dogs, Pepper-spraying Oil Pipeline Protesters." *CBS News,* 5 Sept. 2016, www.cbsnews.com/news/dakota-access-pipeline-protest-turns-violent-in-north-dakota/.

¹⁰ "A Conversation On The Sacred Stone Camp." *It's Going Down,* 4 Sept. 2016, itsgoingdown.org/conversation-on-sacred-stone-camp/.

¹¹ "Dakota Access Pipeline." Dakota Access Pipeline, 30 Jun. 2017, daplpipelinefacts.com/.

"Regulatory Tracker: The Dakota Access Pipeline (DAPL)." Harvard University Environmental & Energy Law Program, 8 Sept. 2023, eelp.law.harvard.edu/2017/10/dakota-access-pipeline/.

¹² Gagnon, Dawn. "Oil Pipeline Protest Draws at Least 150 to Bangor Mall Area on Black Friday." *Bangor Daily News,* 24 Nov. 2017, www.bangordailynews.com/2016/11/25/news/bangor/oil-pipeline-protest-draws-at-least-150-to-bangor-mall-area-on-black-friday/.

¹³ Wong, Julia C. "Police Remove Last Standing Rock Protesters in Military-style Takeover." *The Guardian,* 23 Feb. 2017, www.theguardian.com/us-news/2017/feb/23/dakota-access-pipeline-camp-cleared-standing-rock.

"If you align in any moment with the flow of life as it presents itself, all will unfold in the right way at the right time with a certain spontaneity and ease."

—Tosha Silver

CHAPTER ELEVEN

CLEARING THE DECKS

All the while during Standing Rock, I was also head of my own design firm…! Shocking no one (except maybe me), my business suffered during this time since what was happening with my people took precedence over everything else in my mind, heart, and soul.

By that point, almost all of my business was monopolized by a single client, Catamaran. Even though they weren't my only client when I started, I let them dominate because the money was good and they had a lot of work for us. I built up a full team to handle the workflow as their outsourced design department.

For the first few years, this exchange was mutually beneficial, and we managed things in a reasonable manner. However, Catamaran's female employees, and women associated with them like me, were expected to do the bidding of their male bosses without question or hesitation. So, if an executive had an idea and wanted it by the next day, my liaison, Ella, would be expected to deliver. And I would drop everything to fulfill the demand. Once, the president, visiting from Italy, even came to my office in person so that he could dictate

11 | Clearing the decks

the vision of a design he wanted.

I was still learning to set healthy boundaries. And as usually happened, conditions aligned to nudge me out of a bad situation. Both Grandfather and White Wolf saw my predicament from a higher perspective. "Enough was enough," they're saying, and circumstances were adjusted for me.

A new boss was hired. He frequently yelled to get his way. And if I couldn't deliver, Ella would bear the brunt of it. She and I had worked together and been friends for years, so I went out of my way to help her.

Then Catamaran was sold to a larger company. The new ownership decided to bring their design work in-house.

In the meantime, I had no warning of their intentions. I continued working as I always had, but the breakdown in communications was undeniable. The work from Catamaran started to slow, ultimately dwindling to such a trickle that I ended up dismantling the team, reducing it to a single designer under me.

Obstacles to the trip out west were being removed, one after another. Where work had been all-encompassing, now there was hardly any. Before Catamaran's transition, I couldn't have even taken a vacation for longer than a week, let alone embark on a trip with no return date!

That, however, presented another obstacle. *What do I do now with no money flowing in?*

I shared the whole story with my dear friend Cherie about White Wolf, his sacred object, and the ensuing trip to return it to where it belonged. When I confided my concerns about affording such a trip, she leapt into action. Fully supporting the endeavor, Cherie encouraged me to raise money for the trip. She interviewed me and set up a

11 | Clearing the decks

GoFundMe page.

"You had to learn to have faith in us and trust so that you could make this trip out west without question," Grandfather says.

Even though obstacles were removed one after another, I still had a lot of anxiety about going out west to places where I had never been, let alone being solely guided by Spirit. So, I projected that anxiety onto my husband, worrying about leaving him alone while I made this journey.

"Are you going to be okay with this?" I asked Damon. "I might be gone for as long as six to eight weeks. I don't know how long this is going to take!"

And all he said was, "Yup."

"You're sure?"

"Yup."

"You know, I have no choice. You were there when I rescued it!" I continued to defend my decision to leave… even though he seemed to be putting up no fight whatsoever. "It's been a 10-year journey."

Unperturbed, he repeated, "Yup. Do what you gotta do."

Damon gave me just the support I needed at the time. In actuality, it couldn't have been easy running the farm without help. But he never said a word about it.

One by one, every reason and excuse for not traveling, however long it would take, was removed. An epic clearing of the decks allowed me to make the journey to South Dakota.

"Go forward with courage. When you are in doubt, be still, and wait; when doubt no longer exists for you, then go forward with courage. So long as mists envelop you, be still; be still until the sunlight pours through and dispels the mists— as it surely will. Then act with courage."

—Chief White Eagle, Ponca Chief

CHAPTER TWELVE

WHERE PAST AND PRESENT MEET

Realizing the anxiety was mine, not Damon's, I went into my medicine wheel to pray.

As I sought guidance and sat in ceremony, Grandfather said to me, "Granddaughter, do not be afraid of this journey, for it will take you back home."

As he said this, the sun broke through the trees and lit up my entire medicine wheel. A hawk screeched overhead. The signs demanded, *Pay attention.* I thought he meant my Blackfoot territory. He went on to clarify:

"Along the way, you will find yourself in the place where the massacre you remember from your past lifetime occurred."

My mind reeled at this information. My earliest memories as a young child were recurring nightmares, not of this lifetime: me, running… always running desperately for my life. I would wake up screaming. It felt as if I ran from that lifetime into this one.

After my awakening in Maine, I researched true history, not the version taught in school. I came across descriptions of the atrocities at

12 | Where past and present meet

Sand Creek in Colorado. The mutilations of Cheyenne and Arapaho women and children struck such a deep chord with me that I connected the massacre with my earliest memories. I had convinced myself that this was the event I remembered in my nightmares.

But I wasn't traveling through Colorado on this trip.

Grandfather continued, "I am not going to tell you where that is right now, only that when you find yourself there, you must take the piece of your soul back that was lost at that time. You will need this piece of your soul reunited so that you can move forward in this life to fulfill your purpose and to heal what's been done. Not just for you but to help many others to heal from the past as well."

With Grandfather's words, I knew I must have been incorrect in my original assumption. *Where was I going to find myself?*

For the moment, I had to put my questions aside. I had a lot to prepare for this trip. I had never been away from home for that long and had a lot of logistics to attend to.

"Listen, learn, and witness," Grandfather reassured me.

It still remained a mystery how I was getting to South Dakota in the first place. Until that is, I got a call from my friends Maya and Beth from Sweetgrass Arts.

12 | Where past and present meet

"The unseen is not the unreal, but only that which is beyond our understanding, and that the truth of life is not found in knowledge, but in something close to prayer."

—Kent Nerburn

CHAPTER THIRTEEN

UNEXPECTED MEETINGS

Experiences and meetings are like beads on a necklace. They seem to string together in a pattern that is not recognized until it's done. Another aspect of my business and self-expression was through art, clothing, and stone sculptures. Several times a year, I would vend at different events.

I remember setting up my booth the first summer I was accepted as a vendor in 2016, at a large pow-wow in Connecticut. Two cheerful women were in the booth across from me with a banner that read "Sweetgrass Arts." They run a nonprofit that raises money for the Lakota tribe living on the Cheyenne River reserve. I admired the silver work in their beading and started a conversation that lasted throughout the weekend. We went back and forth to each other's booths, buying, selling, talking, and helping each other throughout the event.

Meeting Beth and Maya that day, who could have known that one day we would be like-minded sisters, drawn together on life's journey? We met up again at many events over the course of years. That first day, we were randomly set up near each other... or were we? I knew it

13 | Unexpected meetings

was no accident; the placement of our booths was divine intervention.

Then, Standing Rock happened.

Maya and Beth went to support their people from the Cheyenne River Reserve. I had artwork flow through me for the protection of the water and the protesters. That artwork and the events at Standing Rock took our friendship to the next level. Maya, Beth, and I became sisters in spirit that year.

When I reissued my first book in the fall of 2018, I had a strong sense that I wanted to create a special edition and donate some of the proceeds to their efforts in support of those on the Cheyenne River Reserve. It just felt right; there was a deep knowing of something more to come. I told Beth's mother, Kay, the founder of Sweetgrass Arts. She thanked me with tears of joy and love in her eyes as she told me this story.

"A kinship developed between me and a Lakota woman who lived there," Kay said. "Our friendship grew strong over the years. She asked me to help her people. And that's when Sweetgrass Arts was born."

Fast forward to the following spring, I received a call from Beth inviting me to join them to travel to South Dakota! They were sponsoring a trip to the Cheyenne River, and because of the donations I had made with the book, they welcomed me as a guest, free of charge. I just had to pay for my flights.

Beth had no idea I was being called to the Black Hills to return the pipe. Her invitation answered how and when I was getting out to South Dakota. It was then that I knew everything was being orchestrated for me.

I accepted their invitation with surprise and gratitude. "Come up to my medicine wheel to pray with me. I need to tell you a story."

My very next call was to Tala. "It's happening. I'm coming out,"

13 | Unexpected meetings

I said, giving her the dates. My heart beat fast with anticipation. I was overcome by a feeling of awe and surrealness as this all unfolded.

The previous fall, my adopted Nipmuc daughter Giselle and I had gone to a sweat lodge we frequently attended. There, we met Tala, who, by a synchronous chain of events, was out from South Dakota visiting her family. She desperately wanted to attend an authentic sweat lodge. Somehow, by word of mouth, Tala ended up connecting with the lodgekeeper and was invited to attend.

After the sweat lodge, during the feast, we were getting to know her. We both felt a strong sense of kinship with each other. I shared with her a short version of the story of the sacred object.

"When it's time for you to come out to the Black Hills, you'll come out and stay with me," Tala said instantly. She lived in Custer, right in the heart of the Black Hills of South Dakota. (No accident there!) She added, "I will help you figure out where to put it to rest if you haven't figured it out by then." She and I became fast friends and conversed on the phone often after that.

This is really happening! I kept telling myself. The logistics were coming together: I would travel with Beth and Maya for one week, then spend a week or however long it took with Tala. And then I planned to travel through Montana to Alberta, Canada, to my ceremonies in Blackfoot territory.

"Goodbyes are only for those who love with their eyes. Because for those who love with heart and soul there is no such thing as separation."

—Rumi

CHAPTER FOURTEEN

THE SACRED EXCHANGE

It was June of 2019, and I was about to leave for… somewhere in the Black Hills of South Dakota. Over the years that his pipe was in my care, I had developed a relationship with White Wolf. And now, I had a bittersweet feeling of saying goodbye as I brought his bundle into my wheel one last time to pray before it went cross-country.

I went into my wheel to pray and had a vision. White Wolf introduced me to his wife, Sun on the Water. They gave me a loving look of gratitude, and I felt deeply touched. I was on a horse with them, on a journey. They said that they wanted to give me a gift. Sun on the Water put something around my neck. "The gift," she said, "will come later. We are of the same tribe but a different band."

In the vision, they took me into the lodge for our final ceremony. I understood that she was Lakota, and he was Cheyenne. This is what I thought they meant, about being of the same tribe but a different band. The prayers were good, and I felt humbled. I teared up as I sat in what felt like a state of grace and felt their gratitude and love.

14 | The sacred exchange

"We will meet again when you cross," they said together. "We will meet you."

Then I saw the warriors line up on horses, the same ones who went with me to rescue the pipe. I was told that some would watch over the pipe, and some would stay to protect me.

As sacred objects, I couldn't take White Wolf's bundle on the plane with me, nor the items I needed for Ceremony when I got to Alberta. Beth of Sweetgrass Arts was also flying, but Maya was driving across the country with a group of young people. I asked if she would accept the responsibility of taking these objects with them. I would trust no other but her. She humbly agreed.

We arranged to meet the week before our departure. I drove down to Connecticut so that I could hand her the bundles. We both felt the enormity of the transfer. Maya had tears in her eyes as did I, as I let White Wolf's sacred bundle out of my care and into her responsibility. She felt the weight and power of it; she was honored to be the one tasked with driving it across the country.

I saw warriors leave with her as she drove away.

I cannot put the profound feelings I felt into words as I held the bundle one last time, thinking of all I had learned these past 10 years. I felt the energy of love swirl around me and embrace me. "As I journey forward, I will not be afraid of what is to come," I wrote in my journal. "This journey, far from home… Or to a home from long ago?"

"They tell me I was a young girl who died in a massacre," I wrote. I remember running in a massacre in my earliest memories. But I didn't know that I did it as a young girl. "I will sense where. I will be shown. I will be home once again and whole from the healing that is to come."

14 | The sacred exchange

"Trust. Have faith," Grandfather said. "You are guided, you're protected, you are loved."

"Hold on to what is good, even if it's a handful of earth. Hold on to what you believe, even if it's a tree that stands by itself. Hold on to what you must do, even if it's a long way from here. Hold on to your life, even if it's easier to let go. Hold on to my hand, even if someday
I'll be gone away from you."

—Crowfoot, Blackfoot warrior

CHAPTER FIFTEEN

BEAR BUTTE AND CHEYENNE RIVER

Earlier that year, almost as a premonition, I started to have severe lower back pain. It came out of nowhere and seemed to heighten whenever I drove in a car. I remember lying in pain in January, staring at the sacred object and saying, "I don't know how I'm going to get you home. I know it's been ten years, and I know I'm tasked with this mission, but I have been out of work, and now I've hurt my back for the first time in my life! I'm at a total loss."

That's when I surrendered, and prayed. I wasn't sure how I was going to drive across three states once I got out West, but I was going anyway. In my journal, I wrote, "I'm in awe of life, and I'm actually going on this journey. It's really happening… Somehow, someway. And now the journey has begun!"

I flew into Rapid City—and just happened to end up on the exact same flight as Beth. Maya met us at the airport and reunited me with everything she carried for me. We settled in, then went directly to the community center at the Cheyenne River Reserve to meet the elders and families. I felt very welcomed and immediately started

15 | Bear Butte and Cheyenne River

chatting with some of the women elders.

The first event on the Sweetgrass Arts group itinerary was to hike Bear Butte the next morning. The elders were very intrigued about my journey and shared some information about Bear Butte so that I could have an understanding of this place, sacred to them, before arriving.

The next day, as we gathered to carpool to the sacred site, I met Wallace. He shocked me right out of the gate by announcing to the group who he was and that he participated in Ceremonies. I was taught that you never tell anyone if you participated, for that is something you hold close to you as work done for the Creator. With his background, I thought perhaps I would sense an energetic kinship between us, but felt resistance instead. This intrigued me, and I stood back and listened and observed as Grandfather had advised. When Wallace ended up in the same rental car I was driving, I was not surprised. He did not know about my mission or my reason for being there, and that was fine with me.

As we pulled onto the road that led to the parking area at the base of Bear Butte, there stood a majestic bull bison not ten feet from our car. I had heard enough stories about not petting the "fluffy cows," so I sat in the car for a moment. Wallace jumped out with his drum and started to sing to the bison. *Well, you must know what you're doing*, I thought, and slowly got out of the car to take photos. I also figured that if the bison charged, Wallace was first in line! The bison looked at me peacefully, and I knew this was the first sign of the trip: a welcome from the ancestors.

The bison never moved, and we left him alone and pulled into the parking lot. I wore a backpack in which I carried the sacred object; I felt strongly that it was important to have it on my person

15 | Bear Butte and Cheyenne River

wherever we went. I did not know where Spirit was going to guide me to put the sacred object to rest.

Since I had that particular issue with my lower back, the hike to the top was hard, but I pushed on. We were not yet in the Black Hills, but it was such an accomplishment to be where we were, that I felt tremendous awe at how the trip had come together. There I was, hiking this sacred mountain I had only ever read about, with the sacred object I'd been the custodian of for ten years on my back. I shook my head and chuckled to myself, *You can't make this stuff up.* Life is more magical than I could ever have thought possible. The beauty and vastness that I witnessed that day as I crested the top of the mountain took my breath away—literally, because I was so out of shape, and figuratively, because it was so beautiful.

That was the first of many hikes I would make on the trip, and I already miss being able to make those amazing hikes at those elevations. By the end of the trip, I felt so healthy from all the climbing.

That evening, Beth, Maya, and I snuck away from the group to meet up with Billie, a beloved elder they'd known for years, for an impromptu visit. He shared many stories that evening, but the one I heard so clearly and understood so well is the one he shared about the seventh generation. It was my first time meeting him and the first time I heard the whole prophecy. Billie was unaware that I was Blackfoot, and that I was the seventh generation. His words validated my story.

The week we spent at Cheyenne River felt like we were pulled out of time, as if time paused and every nuance heightened. Sitting in, just being with the people, doing crafts, getting to know them, and becoming relatives felt so right. Someone asked me to paint two 4' x 8' plywood sheets for them to use as a windbreak around the fire.

15 | Bear Butte and Cheyenne River

I was excited to do so and went to work on the art that I would create for them.

As I painted a four-direction shield on one, a car pulled up with two Lakota women. They got out of the car and stood there sizing me up and watching me for quite a long time. I assumed they thought I was just another white woman from the group when one of the women asked haughtily, "Hey. Do you know what our Ceremony is?"

She named it out loud, testing me. I said, "Yup." And kept on painting with my head down. Not to be rude, but I was concentrating on what I was doing, and I didn't want to engage her any further in conversation. I didn't like where this was heading.

She plowed ahead and said, shocked and sarcastically, "You do?"

"Yup," I reiterated, trying to stay neutral and dissuade her inquiry.

Then she proceeded to do something I know was wrong from all the teachings that I've received from my ancestors. She had no idea who she was speaking to, and yet, she grabbed her left t-shirt sleeve and yanked it up defiantly to show me her upper arm.

Shocked, my mind reeled. Internally, I asked Grandfather, *How should I respond to this? Do I show her?*

"Absolutely!" he volleyed back. He wanted to teach the woman a lesson then and there.

I stopped painting and walked up to her with no expression on my face. As I reached her, I lifted my t-shirt sleeve to show her I was a sister, with the same markings from Ceremony on my arm. The shock on her face when she realized what she had just done left her speechless.

She tripped over her words, almost not making sense, "How are you a…? Where?" She thought she was schooling an outsider, but

15 | Bear Butte and Cheyenne River

knew at that moment that she had offended Spirit instead.

She and her friend ran, jumped in her car, and took off. I never knew what her name was, and never saw her again. The whole encounter left me with mixed feelings. As I pondered what happened, Grandfather said to me, "This was teaching her not to judge others. Let it go; you did nothing wrong. For I told you what you needed to do."

As if to show me the total opposite, the next day, I met the gentle Lakota horseman Shay. Meeting him was like meeting a younger brother from long ago. He came bringing a small herd of horses so that we could ride. How I would have loved to stay the summer and just sleep under the stars and ride horses with him, remembering the freedom of riding on open lands as our ancestors did.

The first horse I learned to ride on was a white pinto. She had died recently, and I was grieving the loss of her. Shay brought a white horse that looked just like her, and I had to get on her back. Once I did, tears ran down my cheeks as I remembered her. He just looked at me curiously, and I explained.

"I lost a horse too, so I know how you feel," he said with a caring demeanor as he shared his story. Shay guided the white horse as I sat comfortably atop her. It was a precious, heart-connected moment.

"Relax, my daughter," Grandfather comforted me. "It's going to be ok."

Each night after our excursions of the day, Maya, Beth, and I would come back together in our shared room and rehash all the magical interactions we'd had. Enjoying each other's company, laughing, and sharing our individual experiences was one of the highlights of the trip.

At the end of the week, our Sweetgrass Arts group left the

15 | Bear Butte and Cheyenne River

Cheyenne River Reserve and sadly said goodbye to our friends. As a last hoorah, we traveled west to the Black Hills. As I took the vastness of it all in, I realized that the majority of the Black Hills had many tourists. At first, this concerned me, seemingly impeding my mission. I set my worries aside, however, reminding myself that the entire trip was Spirit-guided. I would be told what to do, where to go, and how to do it. My only job was to keep putting one foot in front of the other.

At the airport, I saw my Sweetgrass Arts friends off. I felt butterflies in my stomach as I watched Beth board her plane and Maya drive away with the last of the troupe. I was now completely on my own. Custer, South Dakota, was my next clear destination, to join up with my friend Tala, but other than that, I had little idea how the rest of my trip would unfold.

With a bit of fear and excitement mixed into one, I picked up my rental truck and proceeded to travel the unfamiliar roads with trust in the guidance I was getting.

My heart beat fast as I drove. I knew I was getting closer to fulfilling my original mission and reason for being there... Things just got real!

15 | Bear Butte and Cheyenne River

Bear Butte, South Dakota.

Do not pet the "fluffy cows."

"In the moments you think nothing is happening, everything is happening."

—Grandfather

CHAPTER SIXTEEN

THE BLACK HILLS

By the time I reached Tala's home, I was exhausted. "The Black Hills will do that to spiritual people," she said. "Force them to rest because of the change in energy here."

True to her words, just 24 hours later, I felt completely transformed and rested. I shared White Wolf's story. "Did you ever look him up on the Internet?" Tala asked. "See what he looked like?"

"No, it never occurred to me," I said, surprised. "There were so few photos back then, I didn't even think I'd find one."

That morning, I was astonished to find a photo of White Wolf. He was powerful and peaceful at the same time, with love radiating from his eyes. I felt even more determined to find the right place to put his pipe to rest. I figured it would have to be somewhere remote or on private land because everywhere you traveled in the Black Hills, there were tourists. I did not want to risk this sacred object ever being disturbed again.

Tala and I sat in circle that day, making prayer ties and flags and wrapping White Wolf's pipe in bison hide. In a vision, I saw the place where the pipe would be laid to rest. "I saw a small stone cave and a cliff overlooking the land," I described to her. "There was a pile of stones."

A look of recognition came over her face. "I know exactly where that is," Tala said. We packed up and made our way to it. As we traveled, Tala explained how she knew the place in my vision.

"I owned a white wolf." She paused, and we exchanged shocked expressions as the impact of her words landed. "Jynx was a mix, mostly wolf; her father was a timber wolf, and her mother was a red wolf and malamute mix. She died last year, and her grave is on my friend's property."

Tala didn't tell me where we were heading until we pulled into a familiar driveway. I looked at her, confused. I'd literally just come from there! I had stayed in this place the prior night, at the home of Tala's friends, Raya and her husband. Raya participates in ceremonial activities with Tala, walking the same road.

"This was where Jynx was buried?!" I exclaimed, connecting the dots.

Tala had arranged for me to stay with Raya and her husband before traveling on to Custer, breaking up the long and tiring drive. Arriving at night and leaving the next morning, I'd only had time to get to know the warm couple, not their land. I resonated deeply with them. Their house was beautiful and welcoming. I immediately felt at home. It seemed like Grandfather dropped me into these little safety zones along the way so I could rest as I traveled.

As Raya showed me the property on this second visit, she walked me up a hill to a cliff. When I reached the top, I realized that it overlooks a famous landmark. Things seemed even more divinely orchestrated when I saw the cave from my vision. I knew I was nearing the right place but hadn't quite pinpointed the exact location. Then I saw where Tala had buried her wolf, and felt the sacredness and rightness of that spot. White Wolf approved.

"The bundle will be safe here and will not be disturbed," he confirmed. "You can trust this couple to do right by me. They are of good heart."

I was comforted that it was someplace familiar, but also stunned; I knew it would be a huge responsibility for Raya and her husband to undertake, protecting land that would become sacred once the burial took place. They would never be able to sell the property or leave it to just anyone; ultimately, someone would have to carry on that same responsibility. We needed to speak with the couple and make clear what we were asking first.

"Of course," Raya said. She and her partner felt blessed to be asked and to be involved in such a sacred undertaking. As we planned a ceremony for the next day, a huge rainbow appeared over the Black Hills, confirming that this was the right place. My doubts were gone.

The next morning, Tala and I traveled to the top of Coolidge Mountain to pray in preparation. The view was breathtaking. It was an emotional day for me. I thought that my relationship with White Wolf might be ending, and I didn't want to say goodbye, but I also knew that it was time for his bundle to rest. As we drove back from the park, we saw two bison, who seemed to represent White Wolf and his wife. I can not describe the ceremony that we performed that day, but I can tell you about the vision I had when it was over.

After the last white quartz stone was placed on the site, Tala and the others went into the house while I sat alone. Suddenly, I saw White Wolf and his wife and all the warriors who had escorted me on that first day to retrieve what was taken. They encircled and blessed me as I sat immersed in awe.

"I am grateful," White Wolf said. "You fulfilled what I asked of you."

"I will walk with you in your life and watch over and protect you," he continued. "You are now a relative to us."

Grateful tears flowed as I realized I wasn't losing White Wolf's guidance after all.

Then, in the back of my mind, I started to wonder... *When would I be at the place where I died in the massacre? Maybe as I traveled from here? Or in Montana?* But for the moment, I put those questions aside as I sat in the completion of my mission and experience with White Wolf.

The ten-year journey was done. I was at peace in my heart over how it all came to pass.

16 | The Black Hills

"When people come back to their heritage, when they learn their language, when they march to reconcile a part of history that has never been acknowledged, they are slowly putting together the pieces of their lives like a puzzle."

—Rev. Clifford Canku, Dakota Elder

CHAPTER SEVENTEEN

WOUNDED KNEE

The next morning, as we drank our coffee, Tala asked, "So, what do you want to do today? Would you like to go to Hot Springs?"

"Absolutely," I said without hesitation.

"On the way, we can stop at the Wounded Knee Memorial," she added matter-of-factly.

"No!" popped out of my mouth so strongly and defiantly, it surprised us both.

Tala gave me a funny, quizzical look. "Why?" she said slowly. A psychic in her own right, she started picking up on something I wasn't ready to see myself.

"Nope, not going there." The words came from a very deep place in me, but I didn't have any explanation for my friend.

"We have to drive by there to get to Hot Springs," Tala tried to rationalize with me.

"No!" I said again. After some back-and-forth, however, I finally relented because of my desire to go to the hot springs.

Everywhere in this flat country feels like forever to get to, a stark contrast to what I was used to in New England, where trees break up the distance. The flatness is deceptive; places that look close are actually miles and miles away. It was beautiful driving with the view, though, and I took in the vastness of it all.

As we drove onto the Pine Ridge Reservation, I looked over at a hill on my left. Three horses stood in a row, facing west, with a fourth horse down below them in the field. The horse at the head of the row was a white palomino, lit by the sun with its mane flowing in the wind. It was like something out of a movie; so spectacular that it almost looked unreal.

I suddenly realized why I was there. Glancing quickly at Tala, I exclaimed, "NO effing way!"

"Keep driving," she insisted.

My nerves started to get the better of me. I kept saying to myself, "No, this can't be it. This can't be true! The massacre I grew up remembering wasn't here… Can't be this one?!"

I didn't realize I had said some of my thoughts out loud until Tala repeated, "Keep driving."

By the time we reached the Wounded Knee Monument, I was shaking so badly that I could barely get out of the car. Surprisingly, when we stopped, there were no other tourists around, only a single cop cleaning out his car. As we sat there, he finished and drove away.

I gathered myself and walked up to the gate. Tala hung back, giving me space for whatever was coming next. I stood there for a moment, then took off my shoes and reverently walked through. Instantly, I saw the entire massacre happen again in my mind's eye, just as it had occurred that day, December 29, 1890.

I saw my people running. The soldiers cranked the rotating barrels of their Hotchkiss guns, almost like they were new toys they were

17 | Wounded Knee

getting to use. There was much confusion.

I was helping my mother take down the lodge when the chaos started. I was eight years old. I was so bewildered. We were in a peaceful way. All summer we had prayed for others, for healing! *Why would anyone do this?*

Then, I was running and running alongside my mother to get up over the hill and away from the guns. My eyes traced our path as I saw where the ammunition reached us, my mother and me. I remember being shot in the back. We collapsed on the earth, shot and killed just before reaching the crest of the hill. I felt my mother's arms around me as we died in the snow.

I was killed at Wounded Knee. People were screaming everywhere… and then, there was deep silence. When it was over, I hovered over my body. I saw everyone I knew lying there dead. These people, whose hearts had been so full of love, now lay without breath. Soldiers celebrated as though their minds were in a sick way. A sadness for them overtook me as my soul traveled away from that place.

I was transfixed by this vision, reliving it moment by moment. I was there. That was me, lying dead on the ground. My knees gave way beneath me, and I collapsed to the ground.

I lay on the ground, hysterically crying, sobbing, and screaming, all at once. I had never heard those sounds come from my throat. There was a rawness and immediacy I had never experienced in this life. I didn't care if there was anyone around, I didn't care if anyone saw or heard me. I was no longer in current reality.

The unimaginable pain and grief that surfaced penetrated my entire being. As I lay there on the ground, sobbing, I felt something happen. A piece of myself, a piece of my soul that had been buried there, was coming up through the ground to rejoin me. That's when I remembered what Grandfather said, that I would find myself in this place where the massacre from my past lifetime happened.

I recalled his words: "You must take the piece of your soul back that was lost at that time." I knew this was what was happening; I could feel it. Grandfather explained, "The energy imprint of that day for you was still there; this is what I am calling a part of your soul. The oversoul was not shattered, but a piece of your energy from that human life got stuck on that land, because you didn't expect to die that day, so young."

This part of my soul that I lost in that tragic event came back to me in that moment, so I could heal and move forward in my life. I felt the moment it happened; an influx of relief came over me as, for the first time in this lifetime, my soul felt complete.

17 | Wounded Knee

"'People don't understand how hard it is to be Indian,' Carlos said. 'I'm not talking about all the sad history. I'm talking about a way of life that demands your best every single day.... every step you take is a prayer.'"

—Diane Wilson

CHAPTER EIGHTEEN

PRAYING FOR HEALING

I am not sure how long it took for all this to transpire, but at some point, I knew I needed my sage. I needed to smudge and honor all those relatives who died with me that day. I crawled from the ground to my knees and slowly gathered myself. As I walked back to the truck to get my ceremonial things, Tala asked, "Are you OK?"

I'd forgotten she was there. Startled, I answered, "Not yet, but I will be."

Just as I gathered the last of my things to go back into the enclosed fenced area of the monument, two young Lakota girls, who looked to be around 14, came up to us begging for money. Raw and emotional from my remembering, I felt a quick fury rise up inside me. *How dare they disrespect us this way,* I thought. *Begging for money… at our people's gravesite?!*

Speechless as these teens talked to me. I couldn't answer them. Inwardly, I yelled, *You are my relatives! How dare you come to this sacred place to beg for money!*

Tala spoke for me, telling the two girls, "Leave her alone. She's praying."

"Oh, I'll help her pray," one of them quipped in a flip tone.

Tala looked at her sternly. "She does not need your help to pray."

Just then, my eyes met the young woman's, anger seething out at them. The young girls took off so quickly, I don't even know where they went.

Later, I would consider what circumstances might drive such young women to beg, and the danger it exposed them to. At the time, however, I couldn't see past my rage.

Grandfather told me: "You corrected their path at that moment. The look in your eyes jolted them off a dark trajectory. At least one of the girls found the thread to the Red Road and went to her grandmother, asking, 'Teach me what I don't know.'" My ancestors were not the only ones guiding their relatives to heal at that place that day.

I went back through the gates, sat on the grave, and prayed. I prayed for my people, for the healing of what happened that horrible day. I prayed for the souls that were still buried there, that may still be fragmented there. I prayed for healing. I prayed for forgiveness.

I don't know how long I was there; it felt like it was hours before I came back out. I looked at Tala and said, "It's done."

Suddenly, as we were getting into the truck to leave, all these tourists started to show up. I thought to myself, *The spirits were keeping everyone away from this place so that I could do what I needed to do without interruption.*

As we drove off the reservation, I looked to the right. The four horses were now together in a line at the top of the hill. All faced west. The white horse had moved back one position, and the one that had been out of place was now rejoined with the others. I stopped and took a photo; I had to document this moment. These four horses were a

18 | Praying for healing

sign… that I had returned, my relatives had welcomed me home, and the healing had begun.

Later that day, Grandfather remarked, "It was tough to get you to go out west. We have been trying to get you to go out there for a long time. Returning the sacred object was also a mission to get you to go out west for your own healing, for we knew you never would have gone there of your own accord."

"You avoided going out there, even with all the ceremonies you have been involved in. We could not get you to be drawn out there. It had to be your own choice, your own decision, to begin your healing. Your soul is once again whole, and the healing can now ripple out to your people."

Pine Ridge Indian Reservation, South Dakota.

"When you stop making assumptions… your life is completely transformed. Magic just happens in your life. What you need comes to you easily because spirit moves freely through you."

—Don Miguel Ruiz

CHAPTER NINETEEN

MONTANA, BY WAY OF WYOMING

Leaving South Dakota was bittersweet, but I was excited to travel to my Blackfoot territory in Alberta. It was my first time going, so I was still not entirely sure how to get there, but the first leg was clear: get through Montana to the border crossing to Canada.

The night before leaving, a friend of Tala's came over to the house. They talked about the Bighorn Medicine Wheel in Wyoming, which caught my interest. I got a nudge from Grandfather, so I looked it up on the map. In the morning, I was leaving for Montana, and it didn't "seem" very far off my route. Coming from someone who had never before left the East Coast, I now laugh at that. In New England, a 60-mile ride typically takes about an hour. What I didn't take into account was that I would be going up and down mountains and switchbacks. So, a trip I thought would only take a few hours took the entire day.

I left early in the morning, chipper and eager for the next leg of my adventure. Driving alone in a rental truck with not much horsepower, I didn't reach the road that led up to the Bighorn Medicine Wheel until about 5 p.m. I was amazed by how long it took me; I

19 | Montana, by way of Wyoming

kept driving and driving, white-knuckling through the switchbacks... There were parts of the road where nothing separated me from a plunge over the side except a little guardrail.

Arriving at the base of the mountain, I was relieved that it was over (for the time being, anyway). Until I saw a little sign pointing up: all I saw was a one-lane switchback road straight up the mountain! No guardrail, this time.

I sat there, looking up incredulously. "Really? You want me to go up there?!" Alone in my truck, I spoke my thoughts out loud. I was deciding whether it was worth the risk or not to continue up the mountain.

I heard Grandfather say, "Get going," with a laugh.

"Are you sure?" I replied. "That's a one-lane road with no guardrail!"

He just repeated, "Get going."

"OK. Well, I made it this far," I said, resigned.

I drove up carefully, feeling lucky that no one was coming down at the same time that I was going up. Probably because it was so late in the afternoon! When I reached the top, or what I thought was the top, there was a nice big parking area. Seeing other tourists as I parked the truck, I breathed a sigh of relief.

I jumped out and started talking to a woman with her kids who were parked next to me. I asked, "Where is the medicine wheel?"

"It's not much further," she said, looking at me. "It's a mile up that way, and it's a pretty easy hike."

Another mile? I thought. *OMG!* And I shook my head, knowing I had hours of driving still ahead of me after I left here.

I grabbed my backpack and water, and off I went. As I trekked along, taking photos of the amazing scenery on my way up, the hike

19 | Montana, by way of Wyoming

did go pretty quickly. When I reached the top, I felt a sense of reverence come over me. This was a holy place. I could feel the sacredness of the wheel.

As I walked the perimeter of the wheel, I prayed. It was late in the day, and there were very few people there. One other couple was all I saw. Afterward, I was taking a few pictures of the landscape from that high vantage point when a ranger came up to me.

"Please put the camera away," he requested. "There is going to be a ceremony in a few minutes."

"Of course! I understand about not taking photos during the ceremony," I replied as I put my equipment away.

Here I was in Wyoming at sunset, "happening" to be there at just the right time to witness elders perform a pipe ceremony. They had no idea who I was or why I was there. They did not know I was on my way to my own tribe's Ceremonies. I never spoke to anyone. Yet, there I was, praying along with them that evening. It was no accident that I was there. I was guided to be there at just that moment. I think they were Cheyenne. In hindsight, I felt that they had some kinship with White Wolf and his people.

When the ceremony completed, I started making my way back to my truck. I saw a Native woman elder sitting on the edge of her truck bed, waiting for her family to return. She smiled at me with a knowing look. I felt a chill up my back, the kind I get when my soul has been recognized. I saw the light in her eyes as I smiled back. This marked the beginning of something unexpected, a new part of the journey. I was walking into the unknown with no predetermined agenda.

Guided by Spirit (and the GPS), I continued into Montana. One of the things I did not know about Montana is that they don't have street lights on highways, at least not where I was traveling. So

19 | Montana, by way of Wyoming

when it gets dark, it gets completely dark! I had to drive halfway across the state to get to the farm where I had reserved a little sheepherder's wagon for the night.

I called the woman who owned the farm. "I'm running very late."

She said without surprise, "Got stuck in the park, huh?"

"Yep!" I laughed. "I didn't take into account all the ups and downs in the mountains when I was looking at the map."

She clarified the directions on the phone. I prayed I could find her. My hands gripped the steering wheel most of the way.

By the time I got to my host's farm, it was midnight. "You'll know that you turned onto the right dirt driveway when you see the porta john on the left by the barn," she had said. I was completely relieved when I found it on the first attempt.

"Drive straight across the field," she'd instructed, and I did so, pulling in front of an adorable cabin in the pitch dark.

I fumbled my way in with my bag and found a light. My nerves were completely frayed. When I settled in and took in the beautiful cabin with its incredibly welcoming bed, Grandfather said, "You're safe here, you made it. Get some sleep. Good night."

19 | Montana, by way of Wyoming

The Bighorn Medicine Wheel in Wyoming.

Sheepherder's Wagon, Belgrade, Montana.

"Ask questions from your heart and you will be answered from the heart."

—Omaha Tribe

CHAPTER TWENTY

A PROMISE FULFILLED

Such a welcoming place to stay, it was warm and beautiful on the farm. It felt like home, except I was in the middle of Montana on a farm in a sheepherder's cabin. The lovely owner had coffee waiting for me on the cozy deck when I got up. I sat in the sun and took in the amazing property that I found myself on.

Pondering the long drive ahead of me to Alberta, I was still not exactly sure where I was going. My maps gave me a basic idea, but I hadn't spoken to my chief's wife, Naya, since leaving home. Getting a little concerned, I called, trying to catch her that morning. When she didn't answer her phone, I packed up and headed out anyway, in a complete trust fall with Spirit. *So, what's new, right?* At the time, it didn't dawn on me that I wouldn't have cell service for most of the trip. However, I had enough notes to get me going in the right direction.

Praying as I drove, I hoped I was heading to the right border crossing into Canada to get to the reservation. The original plan had been that Naya would wait for me in town before crossing, and I would follow her and the chief the rest of the way. Then, plans changed. Naya had to head home early before talking to me. I drove most of the day with growing concern, until I spotted a sign that read "Cell service ahead" at a rest area turn-off. With a sigh of relief, I immediately pulled in and tried calling Naya, and by the grace of God, she answered!

"Thank goodness!" I blurted before she even said hello. "Am I going the right way?" I proceeded to tell her where I was.

"Yes, keep driving across the border," she confirmed calmly. "Go to the next town and call me back. I will send somebody to get you."

"OK," I laughed as I hung up the phone. *What was I worried about?* I was going to end up where I was going to end up. Even if I had to sleep in the truck, so be it. Knowing I was not in control of any of this trip, I crossed into Alberta and started driving north.

While traveling, my anxiety was heightened, then resolved, each step of the way. Every leg of my journey pushed me past my fear to a new level of trust with Spirit.

After another half-day of driving, I finally arrived at a little town in the middle of nowhere. I called Naya to tell her where I was. "OK," she said, "There's an abandoned gas station at the corner. Wait there, I'm gonna send my daughter to come get you."

Not long after, Naya's daughter pulled in and waved to me to follow her out. I arrived at the reserve at their humble home on this vast plain. I had finally made it and was greeted with such love from both my Blackfoot chief and Naya. It was such a happy moment.

I had been telling them that I would come to their ceremonies for years, once I completed my commitment on the East Coast at my Mi'kmaq territories. And here I was, fifteen years later, fulfilling that promise.

20 | A promise fulfilled

"None of us can ever know what the Creator has in store. Yet maybe, if we return to that circle and that sacred place, we might begin to understand what this existence looks like through the Creator's eyes."

—Wab Kinew

CHAPTER TWENTY-ONE

HOMECOMING

My Blackfoot chief had been instrumental in carrying the ceremonies to our Mi'kmaq territory on the east coast. Every year, he flew out and joined us in New Brunswick, and I looked forward to seeing him. I always knew that these ceremonies were where I was supposed to be, because they represented both of my Native lineages in one place: my Mi'kmaq side and my Blackfoot side, united.

Now, many years later, at the Blackfoot reserve in Alberta, I was introduced to my new "sisters." They showed me around the grounds and where I could set up my tent. I followed each of them around, learning people's names and how they did things differently here, so I would be prepared.

One sister in particular, Aponi, was lovely, and we became instant friends. Aponi and I went out and picked sweet grass. She drove me around so I would become familiar with the area, especially since there were few street signs…! We spent long days together, preparing for the Ceremony and getting to know one another. She was patient and loving in all of my dealings with her.

21 | Homecoming

Finally, the first day of the Ceremony arrived. That morning, as I stepped onto the grounds, I heard Grandfather say to me, "Welcome home, daughter."

"You are the first to be home on our land in seven generations."

My eyes welled up with tears of joy. I felt his love for me in such a deep way as I participated in the ceremonies with my people. I was home.

At the end of the fourth day in Ceremony, I looked up in the clouds and saw a rainbow forming a complete circle over us, almost as testimony. It reflected what I was thinking at the moment, that my journey had come full circle. Not just the journey of this trip, but the journey of my family, and of my life.

This was the end of one stage and the beginning of something brand new.

21 | Homecoming

"Sometimes dreams are wiser than waking."

—Black Elk

CHAPTER TWENTY-TWO

THE LEGEND OF WHITE WOLF

There is always a bittersweet air when our ceremonies finish. The ancestors still linger around us for a time. It is hard to pull myself away from the energies that surround us through those eight days of preparation and Ceremony.

To soften the transition, my Blackfoot chief Ben and I have a yearly ritual of going for breakfast the morning after ceremonies. As I arrived to pick him up, he told Naya, "We do this every year. Want to come along?"

My chief's wife, Naya, is like a second mother to me. She pleasantly declined our invitation, waving us on our way. My chief and I went off for breakfast with a promise to bring her coffee on the way back.

From the moment I met the two of them many years ago, being with them felt like the comfort of family. It was surreal to finally stand in their home, halfway across the country, feeling as at home in the land of my people as I had when I first met them. This feeling of being home was not lost on me; it permeated and blessed my entire stay in

22 | The legend of White Wolf

Blackfoot territory.

Deep in conversation at the restaurant, I realized with surprise that I'd told Ben bits and pieces over the years about my ten-year journey with White Wolf's pipe, but never the entire story, start to finish. So much time had passed, and now, everything had come together. I retold how the pipe came to me, what happened when I put it to rest, and its original owner, White Wolf.

He looked at me with a funny look on his face. "I remember hearing about White Wolf as a child," he said. "There is a legend of White Wolf. His story was used to teach us when we were younger."

"In the time when he was walking this Earth, White Wolf was the only one carrying that name in the territory," my chief continued. "It was said that as a young man, he was on a bison hunt with the men of his tribe when he was knocked off his horse by a bull he had wounded. He stood there, frozen and staring, as the animal turned around, getting ready to charge him. Expecting the end, he started singing his death song."

"As he did this, White Wolf's ancestors came to him. They instructed, *When the bull charges, punch him just above his nose, as hard as you can.* White Wolf gathered his courage as he faced the charging animal. With all his might, he punched the bison just where he was told. The blow startled the beast just long enough for one of White Wolf's brothers to ride up on his horse. Quickly, White Wolf jumped on and was removed from danger."

"The men then took down the bison, and there was much celebration. This story was shared and retold so that young ones would know to listen to the ancestors. That the unseen realm of their ancestors was very real." (And their advice could save your life!)

As I sat listening to Ben, I was blown away. Though many years had passed since a man named White Wolf walked the Earth, my chief's story and my story were connected by this same warrior.

This was deeper validation of all that had happened to me along this journey, and the completion of a circle beyond anything I'd imagined. White Wolf, known for hearing and being guided by his ancestors, had become a teacher and guide to me from the other side. I felt deeply humbled as a wave of gratitude overcame me.

"The cause of human conflict is simple: one person dehumanizes another. One side sees the other side as unworthy. As long as people who disagree perceive each other this way, even the simplest details cannot be negotiated. But let each person bring to the other the attitude of respect and acceptance, and even difficult details can be resolved."

—Paul Ferrini

CHAPTER TWENTY-THREE

TRANSITIONING BACK

It was time to head back. I dropped Ben off at the coffee shop so he could get Naya her coffee while I went to gas up the truck. "I'll meet you in the parking lot," I said.

My errand finished, I waited for quite a while before it occurred to me that it was taking too long. I decided to go in and see what was keeping him.

When I walked in, there was a long line of Natives on one side of the coffee shop. My chief was at the front of it. One woman waited on them while another stood at the other end of the counter. Presuming that one was fulfilling the orders and the other was taking, I figured my chief was next, and we'd be out of there shortly. "I'm going to wash the gasoline off my hands," I called out to my chief.

When I exited the washroom, however, the line still hadn't moved. Without thinking, I threw my hands up and exclaimed loudly, "How long does it take to get a damn coffee in this place?!"

Everyone in line snapped their heads to look at me, astonished. The French Canadian woman on the other side of the counter came to

23 | Transitioning back

life, calling my chief over. "I'll wait on you," she said.

Finally, coffee in hand, we walked outside.

"Do you realize what just happened in there?" Ben asked.

"No, what?" I said, oblivious.

"That woman does not wait on Natives," he explained. "It was only when you spoke to me that she felt safe enough to wait on me." I was floored. That scenario hadn't registered in my mind at all in what I just saw. My innocent reaction disrupted the standoff.

Ben repeated, "Until you came in and talked to me, that woman was not going to wait on me because I was not safe until you spoke to me."

My chief can be an imposing figure at six feet tall, but he is a gentle soul with a huge heart that holds a lot of prayers for many people. It never occurred to me to think of him in any other way.

To witness blatant prejudice was like a slap in the face. It was my first time out west, however. It was a rude awakening and in sharp contrast with the magic that morning had held. It was like being slammed back into the "real world."

My drive away from Alberta overlooked the same majestic mountains I could see from my chief's yard, even though they were clear across the border in Montana. The sacred mountain of the Blackfoot, Chief Mountain, loomed ahead of me. Gathered around it were clouds like puffs of smoke from a pipe.

It was hard to leave this place. It had been such a long journey to get here.

Ben and Naya explained an easier way to get to Great Falls, Montana, where I would return the rental truck and fly home. I had a leisurely drive back and settled into my hotel room.

I had one more day with the truck, and I was looking for some-

23 | Transitioning back

thing to do. I stopped a housekeeper I'd met when I checked in and asked, "Where should I spend my last day here? Oh, and where is a ranch store? My husband asked me to pick up some things for the horses."

She pointed me toward the First Peoples Buffalo Jump State Park. "My son went there on a field trip recently and had a wonderful time. Great vistas to take photos." She also recommended a local ranch store.

The views at Buffalo Jump were breathtaking. I wondered if this place had some connection to White Wolf's story. Signs warning about rattlesnakes gave me a moment's pause, but I trekked on, carefully making my way along the cliffs. I photographed every aspect, enjoying my time alone, reflecting on all the experiences this trip contained.

As this epic journey drew to a close, I felt I wanted to hold onto every detail. Every last interaction rang with significance.

I took my time returning to Great Falls, stopping to take photos along the road until I arrived at the ranch store. When I walked in, I introduced myself to one of the women who worked there, Jolene. "Where can I find a sharpener for horse clippers?"

"I don't think we have any," Jolene said, then looked at me quizzically. "Where have you just come from? I sense a lot of Natives around you."

I was completely thrown off by her comment and answered without thinking, "Well, I just came from ceremonies in Canada. I'm leaving to go back east." We talked for the next two hours as I shopped. I bought a bunch of gifts for my family, the grandkids, as well as the horses. "This is my last stop before I have to drop off the truck at the airport," I explained.

When I got to the cash register, Jolene said, "Give her my discount." The cashier raised her eyebrows, as if to say, *You just met this*

23 | Transitioning back

woman! But Jolene repeated her request.

Before I finished my purchase, she asked, "What are you doing for supper tonight? I'm not done talking to you!"

"I have no plans; I just have to return the truck." I had planned to eat at the hotel, not realizing that it didn't have a restaurant.

"I'll pick you up at the hotel," Jolene announced. "I'm taking you out for supper."

Our talk joyfully continued at a diner that evening. My ancestors were still taking care of me, up to the very last needs of my trip, including a new friend and dinner!

23 | Transitioning back

"The sacred mountain of the Blackfoot, Chief Mountain, loomed ahead of me. Gathered around it were clouds like puffs of smoke from a pipe." Glacier National Park, Montana.

First Peoples Buffalo Jump State Park, Ulm, Montana.

"Healing is not a solitary act. When healing takes place, it has no other option, but to ripple out. It ripples out from the individual into the family, into the community, into the nation, and into the world. Our healing not only reaches forward to our future grandchildren, but it leans backwards simultaneously and grasps, the hands and hearts of our ancestors."

—Helen Knott

CHAPTER TWENTY-FOUR

DID THIS REALLY HAPPEN?

As I settled back into life on the farm, it felt like I was waking from a dream. I experienced magic in almost every moment of my trip.

Why is it that when we're home, in our day-to-day routines, it's harder to recognize the magic all around us? Maybe because it's so familiar. In unfamiliar territory, my senses were on hyper-alert. I was engaged in every moment, every experience, because they were so new to me. It felt like every hair on my head was hypersensitive to the unseen world around me. It was easier to see magic and the sacred in the unfamiliar.

Could I continue to utterly trust guidance from Spirit while at home? If I did, what kind of life could I create for myself and my family? The thought excited and scared me at the same time. The trip felt like a gift: *This is what happens when you have total faith in the unseen world.* I was excited by the possibilities, but the "real" world and financial stresses spun me into another dance with trust. What was in store for me now after such an intense adventure?

"You're never done," Grandfather reminded me. "You're always growing and being prepared for the next version of yourself or life experience."

"You have had to trust the unseen in a way that most people never experience," he continued. "You broke free from fear. When we guided you, you listened and acted. Trust in the unknown is the price, but the rewards are great. Do not worry about how your needs are going to be met, for the worry that enters your body actually pushes the solutions away."

More than anything, I felt like I was being prepared for something even bigger.

Where does Spirit want me to go now? What now?

My experience at Wounded Knee lingered when I got home. The spark that the events at Standing Rock lit... Then reliving the massacre... My bear was seething with injustice. Feelings I didn't have words or context for were now front and center. *Now that I was aware of the anger inside of me, what do I do about it? How can I forgive?*

I asked my Lakota relatives who died with me, "How can I release this anger and hatred towards those who thoughtlessly kill?"

"Are you afraid to die?" they asked.

"No."

"Then picture being in Ceremony and someone shooting you dead in that moment. Who is the victim, really? You, who have now crossed over to the higher realm, which is your home? Or the shooter? The shooter, with his memories of what he has done, is now in a living hell. While you have gone home and are surrounded by your family."

I pictured myself as I am in Canada with my brothers and sisters, and the oneness that we experience. The sacredness we feel together in prayer. In Ceremony, it already feels like we're between worlds, so it wouldn't be that big of a leap to cross over from there. It would feel effortless and natural, not fearful.

They explained to me that had I been killed at Wounded Knee as an adult with this understanding, and not as an eight-year-old child with fear permeating my body, I might have come into this life intact, with a different memory.

Maybe I wouldn't have—painfully, traumatically—left a fragment of my soul behind.

"There is no greater agony than bearing an untold story inside you."

—Maya Angelou

CHAPTER TWENTY-FIVE

HEALING A LINEAGE

It had been three years since my journey across the country to return White Wolf's sacred bundle. Three years since I had reclaimed a piece of my soul at Wounded Knee.

I found myself invited to speak and vend at a new event. As I set up my booth, I was pleasantly surprised to see Callen, a customer whom I had met a few years prior. She was also attending the event.

A couple of days later, it was time for me to give my presentation. Sam, the speaker before me, was talking about healing our ancestral lineage through the body. Intrigued, my friends and I headed over early to catch his talk. When he guided us through an exercise that put my soul sister Cherie, my cousin Wyn, and me together as here to heal our mothers' lineages, I knew then that there was some substance to his work.

My curiosity was piqued—so much so that right after my talk, I went directly to sign up for a healing session with Sam. He was booked solid, so I couldn't get one until the next day. When I inquired about his 1-on-1 sessions, everybody raved about him, but said that he doesn't say anything as he adjusts your body to move and release energy. As expected, when I arrived for my appointment, he gave no explanation or heads up as to what he was going to do.

I had no idea what I was in for.

"Do you want to lie face up or face down?" Sam asked, gesturing at a massage table. I climbed on, fully dressed and unconcerned.

"Oh, I'll lie on my stomach. Face down," I said, following my intuition.

The minute I lay on the table, first thing he did was go straight to the lower left side of my back, the source of my sciatica pain. Shocked, Sam called out, "Callen! Bullet… Wounded Knee! I have to get these bullets out of her back! Can you help me with this?"

I gasped. Sam didn't know who I was. He did not know that I died at Wounded Knee in my past life. I was a little taken aback because I knew he typically worked alone—and here he was asking for help from none other than Callen, the one familiar face I'd seen at the event. "Do I have your permission?" she asked. At the time, Callen did not realize it was me; she just saw a woman on the table. She did not know who I was until the session was complete and I got off the table.

"Yes," I answered, feeling totally fine with that.

As Sam worked to pull the bullets from my energy field, the pain was excruciating, as if I had just been shot. Despite a normally high pain threshold, my lips trembled, and it took everything in me not to cry on his table—or scream! As intense as the sensations were, I recognized that they weren't injuring me; they were releasing the trauma.

That was just the start of my session! Sam walked around me, channeling and carrying on with Callen's support. He guided her where to place her hands on one side of me while he worked on the other. I'm not sure why, but he stepped outside his norm and spoke out loud, sharing what he was getting, to inform me, teach Callen, or for both our benefit.

He placed his hands on the upper part of my back and declared, "Oh my God, you have a huge medicine wheel in your chest. You have an energetic wheel inside you that you can access whenever you need it."

Sam's downloads came hard and fast in a torrent:

"In 1608, you lost everything. In this indigenous lifetime, you lost your farm, your seeds, your animals, your harvest. Everything was stolen and taken from you!"

"Thunder… thunder bolt… You controlled the weather," he said as he worked on my head. "In that lifetime or the next."

Then he picked up on some ceremony I did, "With milk and planting… Planting and pouring milk into the ground, in a dry landscape… Hopi! You were Hopi."

When he got to my feet, he said, "Seven… seventh generation… Blackfoot! Your feet guide you where you need to go. It's like a spider web… a natural GPS system. You naturally know where to go when you travel."

Then, something about ancestors traveling with me in my current incarnation. "Every step you take is guided by your ancestors in this life." Finally, he was done.

He walked away and didn't say anything more. *The session must be over,* I thought. I got off his table. None of this was recorded. I had only my memory to rely on. Fortunately, Callen was there as a witness.

Talk about an intense session! I already knew I was a seventh-generation Blackfoot, but Sam didn't. He picked up on so many things he could never have known or been privy to.

I couldn't speak. The woman who had the next session asked,

25 | Healing a lineage

"How was it?" I couldn't answer her. I walked straight back to my booth in the vending area and ducked behind the tall display. Hidden from view, I sat down and started to bawl. I was overcome by what had just occurred.

My cousin Naomi, who was there tending the booth, came flying around the corner when she heard me. "Oh my God, what happened?!" she cried out, stunned by my sudden, inexplicable distress.

I was totally speechless. The answer would have to come later.

25 | Healing a lineage

"Upon suffering beyond suffering, the Red Nation shall rise again, and it shall be a blessing for a sick world. A world filled with broken promises, selfishness and separations.
A world longing for light again."

—Crazy Horse

CHAPTER TWENTY-SIX

MEETING MY DESTINY… AGAIN

November 4, 2022. I knew something was coming when I walked out of the barn after tending the horses, turned to walk back to the house, and an immense shooting star flashed across my field of vision.

Bigger than I'd ever seen, massively bright, with an electric indigo-blue tail. Awestruck, I felt blessed by its appearance, as if the star reassured me, *everything is going to be okay.* I stood there, breathless and captivated, as I felt awash in the love of my ancestors and Creator, in that brief, magical moment.

It was a beautiful, clear night. As I witnessed this event, I had a feeling unlike any I had ever experienced before. It was an overwhelming feeling of portent as I stood transfixed. A sign? Yeah, it was a sign! Of something huge on the horizon.

Callen called me the next morning. "Are you going?" she asked.

"Going where?"

"To the reparation ceremony at the Barre museum!" She explained, surprised it was news to me. "A small museum in Barre, Mass. They have a huge collection of objects looted from the Lakota who

26 | Meeting my destiny… again.

died at Wounded Knee," a violation of the Native American Graves and Protection Act.[14]

"Years ago, when I lived in Barre, I went to the museum for a workshop on making warm window inserts. A woman from the museum offered to bring me up to the second floor, which was a locked space and very dim and dark with full-length curtains all the way around," Callen continued. "There was a very heavy, dense energy there. There were cases of Native objects all the way around the room. When I saw them—children's dolls, moccasins, sacred objects, even hair—it affected me deeply."

"I didn't ask to see them… They invited me! Anyway, they're giving them back… Finally!" Callen finished. "There's going to be a whole ceremony at the museum to return the items to the Lakota people."

"I had no idea that was even happening!" I said, stunned that it was my first hearing of it. Unsurprisingly, the Barre Museum story hadn't been picked up by bigger media outlets, which was part of why I hadn't heard about it. "I have to be there… I died there! Those could be some of my things, my family's things!"

"And that is why I'm calling you," she said. We made plans to meet at the event.

This is the beginning of the reparation, I thought on my drive up. It was the start of making amends, healing the massacre of my people. Acknowledging that it even happened. *Yeah, this is big. This is part of my destiny, part of the reason I am back living as a human on this Earth. I ran for my life in that massacre, practically running from that life into this one.*

I had a deep realization… *I am back to represent those who died alongside me on that horrible day.* To speak for the people who are not seen, heard, or remembered, even today.

As I got closer to the venue, my anxiety rose in anticipation of seeing the items taken from us. I got choked up in the car as I spoke out loud to my ancestors, asking for their help and guidance.

The emotions were about to overtake me and send me back home. Just as I thought, *I can't do this,* a bald eagle swooped low over my car, in plain sight. Not ten feet from me, on a highway I travel often, where I'd never seen an eagle before. I could see every feather in stark relief against the bright blue sky. My ancestors sent it to comfort me. Encouraged, I kept going.

Interesting that I had only become aware of the event that morning. Had I known what an ordeal this was going to be for me, I probably would have resisted more. It was hard enough to keep driving with all the feelings rushing through me. My ancestors did not want to give me much time to think about it before committing to attend. In a way, they tricked me into going! If I'd had too much time to think about it, I might not have gone at all. The emotions would have proven too much. *Could I keep it together in public?* I thought.

When I arrived, the heavy burden I saw on the faces of my Lakota relatives told me that I wasn't alone.

---

[14] Angeleti, Gabriella. "Massachusetts Museum Accused of Hoarding Indigenous Artefacts and Human Remains for Decades." *The Art Newspaper,* 1 Apr. 2022, www.theartnewspaper.com/2022/04/01/massachusetts-museum-accused-hoarding-indigenous-artefacts-human-remains.

26 | Meeting my destiny… again.

Shooting star simulation on an actual photo taken the evening of November 4, 2022.

26 | Meeting my destiny… again.

"An estimated one million Native American remains were held in public and private institutions by the late 1900s. That is, however, a conservative estimate, considering the vastness of private collections and the remains that have been shipped to Europe, Japan, and elsewhere."

—Winona LaDuke

CHAPTER TWENTY-SEVEN

THE REPARATIONS CEREMONY

Two long tables stood at the front of the room, separated by a podium. Museum staff sat on the left while Lakota Sioux sat on the right. Media and onlookers crowded front and center. I felt drawn to the far side of the room, away from most of the spectators. I did not want to be in the spotlight, but I had to be close to the people and objects that meant so much to me. I chose a seat in the front row.

A press release described the event this way: "About 150 items considered sacred by the Sioux peoples that have been stored in a small museum for more than a century are being returned... The items include weapons, pipes, moccasins, and clothing, seven or eight of which are thought to have a direct link to the 1890 Wounded Knee Massacre."[15]

There were a lot more than seven or eight items from Wounded Knee.

I approached one of the tribal members at the far side of the room, Cole. His head bowed and eyes closed, he seemed overcome with emotion. He looked so familiar to me, I felt compelled to introduce myself anyway.

27 | The reparations ceremony

"Hi… are you from Green Grass?" I had been to that reservation in 2019, and thought maybe I saw him there.

"No, Rosebud," he said gruffly, dismissing me. Which made more sense, as Rosebud borders the Pine Ridge reservation, where Wounded Knee is located. In hindsight, I suppose that Cole must have thought my question came from ignorance, not recognition. He probably looked familiar because of my past lifetime. In the end, I walked away and let him be.

As I sat there taking everything in among the representatives and family members from Pine Ridge Reservation, I felt like a living ghost. Those gathered did not realize that one among them, an unassuming presence, was a living witness to that horrible day, December 29, 1890.

I choke up as I write this because how can I even describe the feelings? The items that Cole was now responsible for carrying in Ceremony belonged to our related families—his grandfather's and my mother's. Though he did not recognize me, I was a relative who died that day at eight years old, returned. It felt like timelines colliding.

With the restored items, my people could now mourn those of us who perished and properly lay us to rest. We could all be together in our sorrow and move on. There were my relatives, grieving our loss, not knowing that I was there alongside them, present but hidden like a spirit.

Throughout my experience, with her smiling eyes and humor and radiant love, my spirit Lakota grandmother was supporting me in the background. And now, through this reparations ceremony, the unseen world met the seen, as sacred objects were returned to living descendants, and as my soul was again connected with my blood relatives from my last lifetime.

All were completely unaware—but one. One person noticed me,

the Lakota woman sitting just one row behind me.

---

[15] Pratt, Mark. "Sacred Items in Barre Library's Museum to Be Returned to Sioux." *The Worcester Telegram & Gazette,* Associated Press, 11 Oct. 2022, www.telegram.com/story/news/2022/10/11/native-american-artifacts-barre-museum-returned-sioux/10463714002/.

"Healing comes when the individual remembers his or her identity—the purpose chosen in the world of ancestral wisdom—and reconnects with that world of Spirit."

—Malidoma Patrice Some

CHAPTER TWENTY-EIGHT

AVA

Ava insisted on representing the women. As she walked up to the podium to speak, there was thick silence in the room left by the prior speaker, who took us into the heart of why we were all there: the tragic story behind the items being returned.

This petite woman peeked over the mic, looking very serious. "Testing!" she said abruptly in a soft, jovial voice. We all laughed as her unexpected humor broke the heaviness in the room. In that instant, I knew why she had caught my attention. With her twinkling eyes, Ava looked exactly like my spirit grandmother.

When the transfer ceremony was complete, I watched the Lakota representatives wrap star quilts around the museum board members, recognizing them as one of the first museums to return sacred objects to their people. *Finally!* I thought.

Then, the giveaway commenced.[16] It was then that I saw Iris, Nick's daughter, overseeing the giveaway table. The synchronicity wasn't lost on me; Nick had been the Lakota man who hosted the sweat lodge I attended after I rescued the pipe, the first I had asked for advice at the very beginning of this epic adventure.

It felt like a cycle completed this day, from the return of White Wolf's sacred bundle to South Dakota, to the return of sacred objects stripped from the people massacred at Wounded Knee to their descendants.

"Where's your father?" I asked Iris, looking around. "He should be here."

"I don't know. He was supposed to be," she answered.

As the event drew to a close, Ava sat near me and we looked at each other. She said urgently, "I need to speak with you."

"I need to talk to you, too!" I agreed, feeling the same urgency.

Ava remembers differently, that I approached her first. In any case, there was a strong sense of recognition when we saw each other. We were drawn together, and the spirits orchestrated it as it needed to happen.

Quickly, Ava and I hustled to sneak out the back door before she was swamped with attendees who wanted to meet her. We barely made it outside when a woman poked her head around the corner and said, "I just wanted to say hi!"

We looked at her wordlessly until she left. Finally, we were alone.

Ava and I stood there looking at each other. "I don't know how to say this to you," I confessed.

She smiled. "Just say it," she said, reaching out to take my hands.

How do I tell her who I am and why I'm here? I thought. Past rejections by my own people simmered inside me. *Would she judge my light skin? Beyond that, how would I share things I usually kept secret—like past lives and spiritual gifts?*

I stood there for what felt like minutes, struggling internally, until my spirit Grandmother said, "She is family. She needs to know."

Then Grandfather added, "It is time to speak now. Find the courage. Would you drive all the way home and miss this opportunity to reconnect with family because of fear?"

The words spilled out of me as I shared with her who I was and why I was there, ending with, "You look just like my spirit grandmother. She says we are family." Tears welled in her eyes as I spoke. When I finished, we hugged. Ava looked me in the eyes.

After a long pause, she said, "I believe you." I inhaled apprehensively, waiting for the "but" that never came.

Instead, in a hushed tone, she continued, "I believe in reincarnation. Long ago, my great-grandmother told me that our relatives who were killed that day would come back. And that they would come in different bodies and tell us who they are…"

She lovingly smiled, "So, yes, I believe you."

Her words stunned and relieved me. "I knew there was something about you the moment I saw you," she finished.

---

[16] Moreton, Bruce. "The Give Away Ceremony - a Lakota Tradition." Night Eagle Wilderness Adventures, Night Eagle Wilderness, 6 Nov. 2022, www.nighteaglewilderness.com/post/the-give-away-ceremony-a-lakota-tradition.

"It is, simply, a world where everything interacts and everything has power, and our modern rules of cause-and-effect don't apply; where plants have dominion, animals have dominion, trees have dominion—as do wind and water and clouds and spirits; where the dead are always present to guide us...."

—Kent Nerburn

CHAPTER TWENTY-NINE

MY SPIRIT GRANDMOTHER

Two weeks later, I received this message from my Lakota spirit grandmother:

"Granddaughter, your destiny has come to greet you. It is wrapped around you with love, healing, and peace. Feel the presence of your Lakota relatives. We are here with you and surround you, and comfort you in this life. We guide you. We love you, for you are one of us. You are one who lost their life alongside us."

"This morning, we showed you the doll you held that fateful day. We showed you your mother's moccasins." (I had found old pictures online of some of the items from the Barre Museum's collection).

"This is part of your healing process, part of bringing back those pieces of your soul that broke off that day and shattered. That's truly what happened; your eight-year-old self, dying in such a violent way alongside your mother, shattered your soul like broken glass. And now we pick up the pieces in this next incarnation."

"Know that we are with you; know that you are not alone. Our love is wrapped around you. The courage it takes to see who you truly

29 | My Spirit Grandmother

are is huge. Not all of your relatives will recognize you. Many struggle in this world that you live in now, especially those survivors who were left behind to pick up the pieces after such an atrocity."

"You are a living legacy. You have returned, even if some don't understand or even ridicule your story."

"We will protect you. You are leading the way up the mountain, and we are there with you. It is the time for healing and reparation."

29 | My Spirit Grandmother

"Strive for happiness as lesser men strive for power: and remember that love is both the seed and the flower of joy. Let your actions be such that if they were done to you they would increase your happiness. Love others that they may love you: And love yourself that you may love others."

—Joan Grant

CHAPTER THIRTY

LETTING GO

The next morning I got a surprising text from Callen.

"I received a message in a vivid dream this morning from a Lakota grandfather who I have not seen before," she wrote. "He showed me a Split Feather, or a Spirit Feather. One side was see-through and existed in the spirit world, and the other half was white and in the created world."

Her vision led us into a deep phone conversation during which Spirit revealed who she was. I relayed, "Grandfather says there is an important message in the feather dream that you received. What do you think it is?"

Callen was quiet for a few minutes. Her voice cracked as she said:

"I'm getting… I was the soldier who killed you at Wounded Knee."

She started to cry as the full import of her realization landed. She was the soldier who had shot and killed me, my mom, and many more at the Wounded Knee Massacre, reincarnated. She connected the dots, "That's why I had to be there for your healing with Sam… Because I had been the one who put the bullets in your back." Her words slowed as a wave of emotion came over both of us.

My ancestors were adamant about the next step. "You need to come down here today!" I said urgently. "We need to go into my stone circle and do a forgiveness ceremony."

She hesitated. "Give me ten minutes to think about it," she said. As the words left her mouth, with a start, she felt an unseen force physically push her from behind…!

"Never mind! It's a long drive, but I'm on my way!" she exclaimed.

After Callen arrived, we sat down over tea and rehashed the events leading up to this moment. We gathered ourselves, our things, and went to the stone circle to sit in prayer together to do the next right thing for both of us… to heal and forgive. We had a sense, an understanding that it would ripple beyond our individual roles at Wounded Knee. We were surrounded by an intense energy in the wheel. I thought, *Wow, this is happening, and it's happening today.*

Time seemed to slow down. At one point, we heard horse hoofs clip-clopping by on a nearby road. Later, we heard gunshots in the distance! Both unusual sounds seemed directly tied to why we were having the forgiveness ceremony. We looked at each other, shocked. Callen then had a vision of a line of Native women looking at her with a sense of peace about them, acceptance on their faces.

And then, it was complete. A moment later, a red-winged blackbird hung in the air to the west of us, chirping incessantly to get our attention. Looking over at him, we gasped in unison and amazement as a bright sundog, a circular rainbow, showed through the clouds.

With this rainbow, we felt our ancestors' acknowledgement. We knew that the forgiveness prayer was accepted and complete.

Healing our past incarnations as murdered and murderer, child and soldier, we sat together with tears in our eyes and love in our hearts. Karmic ties cleared, we were ready to let go and move forward.

30 | Letting go

"To be alive is the biggest fear humans have. Death is not the biggest fear we have; our biggest fear is taking the risk to be alive—the risk to be alive and express what we really are."

—Don Miguel Ruiz

CHAPTER THIRTY-ONE

THE RIPPLE EFFECT

The warning came from my ancestors in January. I looked down at the carpet and saw a thread of yarn twisted in the shape of a breast cancer ribbon. I noted it but walked away. When one of my granddaughters also pointed it out, that's when I knew it was significant.

Then my dog Mia got very sick. The next night, we rushed her in for emergency surgery. They told us that she had cancer. I told myself, *That was why the cancer ribbon was on the carpet. That's what my ancestors were warning me about.* But no, it was more than that.

Soon after, I had an appointment with my doctor. She asked if I would at least get an ultrasound because I had refused mammograms my entire life. I agreed. Sometime before the procedure, Grandfather asked, "What would you do if you had cancer?"

I didn't hesitate. "I would go to my natural doctor, who's an expert in treating it," I answered. Certified in internal medicine and medical acupuncture, formerly a conventional primary care physician, I trusted Dr. Nate implicitly. "I would go the alternative route. No chemo or radiation. And if it was my time to go, I would accept it."

31 | The ripple effect

When the ultrasound results came back, the letter was distinctly worded so that I would not freak out. It stated that they had found something inconclusive, but not to worry. They recommended I check again in six months.

"No, you have it," Grandfather revealed. "Do not believe the letter. Take this seriously and deal with it now… If you go the natural route you described," he continued, "It will be healed in six months. But if you do nothing, it will have progressed much further, and you will have a more serious battle to face in six months."

In a dream soon after, my ancestors explained, "This illness is an initiation. You need to trust, have faith, and believe, because miracles can happen and do all the time."

"You will be a living witness that a miracle has occurred," they finished.

A few weeks later, I went in for my regular checkup with Dr. Nate. He's known about my gifts for all the many years I've seen him. "My ancestors told me I have cancer," I said simply. I asked him to validate that it was cancer, and he did, and it was.

For the most part, I felt no fear; if there's anything I've learned at all, it's to trust the guidance of my ancestors. My conviction and trust in natural health were strong. Dr. Nate sensed that as well, and he was sure that this was something we could heal. He put me on a hefty protocol of supplements and lifestyle changes.

Certain as I was, emotions crept up as I drove away. I danced between faith and fear. What would Damon do without me, my parents… I wasn't ready to go. Tears flowed because this was another journey I had to undergo to test my resolve and faith.

31 | The ripple effect

"When I let go of what I am, I become what I might be."

—Lao Tzu

CHAPTER THIRTY-TWO

PREPARING FOR WHAT'S NEXT

I chose to tell only a few in my inner circle. My ancestors warned that gossip by anyone who feared losing me would be a huge detriment to healing. Words and thoughts create; I needed to protect myself at all costs. Drama creates more drama.

What I didn't realize was that the healing had already started. I dreamt that my ceremonial brother and sister were praying for me, despite not knowing about my health issue. We have a deep soul connection, so I knew the dream was true. I felt great gratitude toward them.

My first ever mammogram was scheduled. A doctor was present, which was unusual, seeming to indicate the seriousness of the situation. Something got their attention on the results, and they asked me to stay while they got clearance for another ultrasound.

During the ultrasound, as I watched the screen, Grandfather guided me internally, "See that white section they just scanned over? That was it… The doctor missed it. We do not want this in your medical records. It will not be found here."

When the doctor finished, she said, "The tissue configuration of the left breast is completely different than the right." She couldn't make sense of it.

I kept quiet and smiled as Grandfather explained, "The herbs and supplements you are taking are working and healing the tissue. This is why it appears so different."

When another "inconclusive results" letter arrived in the mail, I wasn't surprised. A rescan was set for six months later.

Well, if this is it, how can I prepare? I worried. I came right up against my mortality. I started cleaning up my paperwork and items I no longer needed, giving things away. I made sure to make my final wishes known, rattling off a list to my soul sister Cherie.

I was basically letting go of my past, so I had nothing holding me back and I could meet what my future had in store for me. Things got real… I faced not being here, and what was truly important to me. This was the initiation that my ancestors were talking to me about. After I passed this threshold, if I survived, who would I become?

My husband got quiet while watching me go through this health challenge. Damon was facing his own fears. I was much younger than him; he never expected that I might leave first! This disrupted and affected him deeply in his mannerisms and actions, though he never voiced his thoughts. He supported me the best he could by handling the day-to-day chores on the farm, through this uncertain time. Did he support the holistic route I chose? No, but he accepted that it was the only route I would take. He seemed to hold his breath as he watched me navigate the choices I made.

Before I knew it, it was time for me to get ready to travel again, for an upcoming speaking event. I immersed myself in preparations.

32 | Preparing for what's next

Dr. Eliza, a gifted naturopath I had met at the same event the year before, came to the forefront of my thoughts. She has a deep connection with the angels.

"It will be important for you to talk to her," Grandfather said.

At the time, I had no idea why Grandfather brought her to my attention. I fluctuated between a knowing that what I was doing with Dr. Nate would take care of the healing, but I sensed a more ethereal direction when I thought of Dr. Eliza. Not comprehending anything in the actual moment, I felt strongly that "something" was up in my near future with my meeting her again this year.

At the event, Dr. Eliza and I hugged in greeting. She said, "I was told by Archangel Michael that there were four people whose lives depended on my help here. Then I saw your face in my mind's eye prior to coming."

I shared the health challenge I was facing. She immediately quipped in her Texas accent, "Aw, well, we'll need to take care of that then, won't we?"

The next morning, I went straight to Dr. Eliza for a session. "The angels can heal you if you believe," she proclaimed.

"Oh, I believe!" I insisted. Of course, I believed; I've been seeing angels since I was a child. I trust them—and Dr. Eliza.

"And so it is done," she confirmed. She looked at me and smiled.

I felt an incredible peace settle over me. It really was done! My healing was quick and miraculous. Almost anticlimactic, it happened so fast! I knew without a doubt that this initiation had reached its end. *My body may need a moment to catch up,* I thought, but energetically, spiritually, the healing was complete in that single moment.

I felt filled with joy. I let the reverberations of my healing wash over me for the next few days. In a session later that weekend, a different healer confirmed, "The cancer is completely gone." The swiftness of the miracle and her validation settled my internal voice.

Laughter and happiness filled my soul. I knew that this experience was taking things to a new level for me. I had passed a test, so to speak, and I felt the weight lift from my shoulders. I was back on track and a walking example of a miracle.

I didn't realize how important it was that I believed with total faith until Dr. Eliza shared a story, in contrast, about a previous client in her presentation on the last day of the event:

"A patient got on my table with three huge tumors in her belly, big enough that I could feel them under my hand: one the size of a lemon, one the size of an orange and the third the size of a grapefruit! The angels worked on her. Once she was healed, the tumors were completely gone…There was nothing there, you could feel it."

"Immediately, the patient sat up and said, 'I don't believe it!'"

"The healing started reversing immediately," Dr. Eliza explained. "She came back to get on my table two more times. See, I can't tell her what to do, or say, or not say, because that's not how this works. We always have free will. And the second time, she did the exact same thing. The first words out of her mouth were, 'I don't believe it!'"

"That third time, I couldn't resist, I had to hint at something… After the healing, when she went to sit up, right away, I grabbed her hand and placed it on her belly, so she could feel the miracle. 'Hold on, hold on—maybe this time, you could just take a minute?'"

The healing finally took hold only when her patient learned NOT to say, "I don't believe it!"

After I returned home, I shared the news with Damon. He didn't know what to make of it. His faith was being tested too; this just wasn't how his world worked. I had an appointment scheduled with Dr. Nate the following week. My anticipation was palpable! Would he be able to tell right away? I was excited at the prospect and a bit nervous as well. Would he confirm what I already knew to be true?

When I arrived, I informed him, "The cancer is completely gone." From the look on his face, I could see that he was excited for me, but a little nervous too. "It's ok," I said, "I know you need to test for it to be sure."

Dr. Nate took his time, testing me thoroughly and cross-checking to be sure. When the testing was complete, a slow, triumphant grin spread across his face. He had so many patients he wasn't able to help because they would only come to him as a last resort when the medical path had failed them, not as a first choice, as I had, which was validating for him as well.

"It's totally gone! Nothing is there!" he said ecstatically. This reserved man of science then lifted his arms in a "V" for victory as he literally jumped for joy in celebration with me.

"Humankind has not woven the web of life. We are but one thread within it. Whatever we do to the web, we do to ourselves. All things are bound together. All things connect."

—Chief Seattle

CHAPTER THIRTY-THREE

TRUSTING LIFE

When I initially embarked on this journey, charged with returning the sacred object, I never could have anticipated how it would change my life.

Every soul's journey is unique, personal, and different. Nothing is random. Situations, events, and occurrences happen for a reason. Things that need to be healed come to the surface. The pipe came to me because a wrong needed to be righted. And that was just the beginning...

In my case, the chain of events happened exactly as it needed to for me to find a new way of being in the world. Like any rebirth, allowing and surrendering to a new way of being required me to let go of who I thought I was and allow the unknown future to emerge.

As a collective, this is happening to all of us. We are in the process of birthing a new reality, a new way of being together.

Change is happening faster than ever before. We seem to live more than one lifetime in our current incarnation instead of having to die to be reborn. In prior embodiments, we may have moved through one scenario or lesson over many lifetimes. Now, it's the opposite, as we move through many lessons within a single lifetime.

Or perhaps it's also that our perception has shifted.

Coming home, even though my days looked the same, taking place in the same environment, I was different. I had evolved and continue to grow and change. Nothing was and is the same, because we are always progressing. In truth, we face the unknown every day. It is an illusion to think that we do not.

Before I officially published this book, years after my return from South Dakota, I reached into my cabinet to store the fortune cookie fortunes from that week's trip to our favorite Chinese restaurant. Keeping the little slips of paper in a jar was a tradition I'd started since that first, momentous fortune, "Spirit guides accompany you."

It was after midnight. The painted green cabinet, built in Bavaria in 1840, with glass doors and white ceramic handles, is a time capsule in and of itself. When I opened the doors, a large mason jar hidden behind the central panel, on the middle shelf, caught my eye. I hadn't noticed it for years, as I made my weekly deposit into the fortune cookie jar. Suddenly, it registered that the jar was filled with the tinpsila, or prairie turnips, I'd brought back from South Dakota.

Instantly, I was transported to another time. In my vision, the tinpsila dried overhead as I lay in a teepee. I smelled the smoke from the fire. I sat up and looked across to where I knew my grandmother slept. Seeing me, she called me to her with a gentle wave of her hand. Seeing my grandmother, my eyes filled with tears. Somehow, I knew it to be the summer before Wounded Knee occurred, a time of love and contentment. Strangely still aware of my body in the present, I stood before my kitchen cabinet, one foot in each timeline, bawling. Seeing the turnips collapsed time and space, blurring them together.

33 | Trusting life

Overcome with the connection from the past, with the connection to my Lakota family, my heart flooded with love from them. I could feel them reaching through time to touch my heart, and I felt profound gratitude. Tears continued streaming down my face. Our connection was not destroyed at the massacre; the jar, in that moment, became the most precious thing I owned. It was a portal that reached through time and space to remind me of who I was. And it was just sitting there, all these years, waiting for me to notice—or evolve.

It was the first time I had opened that cabinet since I returned from our Ceremonies that summer, and I was still in a prayerful state, not yet fully returned to my day-to-day reality on the farm. Deeply touched by the experience, I still had a fleeting thought, *Is this real?*

My ancestors answered, as a huge shiver ran down my spine. "If this was not truly your story, if it was not your truth, you would not feel us this way, so deeply," they said. "We know you feel us, and you know we are with you. We are connected always. We were with you when you were praying in Ceremony. That is your tie to who you truly are, my daughter."

As I recorded my experience moments later, they told me that I'd reached an energetic level where they could touch me in a different way, allowing me to feel them in my heart. That, as I grow, the connection between us grows stronger and closer to the surface. It's like my heart expanded with their love.

We create new and evolve with every breath, every decision, and every thought that crosses our minds. Every nudge or sign from Spirit gets us to the next moment and the next creative inspiration or completion of a project.

Life is a walk in faith. I choose to do it consciously, clearly, and connected to Spirit. Creator, our higher self, and those who love us in

33 | Trusting life

the unseen realms can help guide our next step. This is where trust in life comes in. Even those gifted with foresight must have faith in this way.

We can walk through life unimpeded by fear. We can walk through life guided by Spirit and faith, and trust that we are being led in the right direction, toward our mission and purpose.

The journey of our lives can be as exciting or as simple as we choose. The contrast we experience going from times of movement to times of stillness has lessons to teach us.

When we stop and listen to our innermost thoughts, desires, and feelings, we uncover what life is all about: self-discovery and the joy of creating our lives anew in every moment and every circumstance.

A single act, a single healing, a single thought—a single changed perspective—can transform everything.

33 | Trusting life

"Fear and love cannot occupy the same space."

—Grandfather

EPILOGUE

A final word from White Wolf

My first time in the wheel since my health journey, White Wolf joined me in ceremony. These are the words that he shared that day:

"Daughter, Sister, I think of you as family. For you have done so much for me in returning the sacred pipe that I carried, and for knowing how important it was to make the journey out west. And then the gift you received, going out there to receive the part of your soul that was stolen during the massacre. Your life was stolen at that time.

"We want to acknowledge you. We want to give back to you. This year has been a tough transition for you. The gift of the healing you received is a thank you from us as well. We helped to orchestrate it for you. We saw how in despair you were and how hard and heavy this burden had been on you. And we wanted to lift it from your shoulders.

"We want to remind you of the power that is inside you. Not only is the medicine wheel inside you, your pipe is inside you. You also have us surrounding you and walking this path with you. You are not alone. No matter what you face in this life, you are not alone. When you sit in the circle in this wheel, even the elementals here respect you for what you have done. They have watched you over the years that you've lived here.

Epilogue | Returning What's Sacred

And you have garnered much respect. So you don't need to dance every step in life. You have given much already.

"You need to listen to the silence, the birds, the animals. We are all here with you. We're sitting here in ceremony with you. Things are going to change very quickly for you. Know that whatever you need to face, we are with you. We surround you. We walk with you."

"Follow the doors that we open for you along the way. You are to go forward from here. We heard your prayers. All who you love are in your heart, and you are in theirs."

"So just take things as they come. For nothing stays the same. And what is waiting for you is, of course, a wider berth. Well, let's say we have a bigger mission for you. You answered our call, and there is no greater power than that love. Love is what connects you. Creator's love is what connects us all."

"You understand that, and strive for oneness. Striving for balance is also important at this time. Yes, change is coming. You will witness it. And from there, everything will be different."

"We want you to know how grateful we are to you. We want you to know that we understand how grateful you are as well. You do not have to keep saying it to us, we know, we feel it in your heart. Our love for you is as strong as your love for us. There is no beginning or end to love. And as the peaceful warrior that you are, as you walk on this Earth in human form, there is much to do. You working in conjunction with us is more than we could ever ask for."

"We are truly proud of you. Be well, my sister. Go forward from this point on, knowing that we walk beside you. Knowing that all the warriors that you've helped, all my warriors, your fellow warriors and your family, all walk beside you, with you.

"With much love, White Wolf."

AN OFFERING

The simplicity, by Marie Dion

God is found in the simplicity of everything.

In the light that shines through the crest of a wave,
in the love that shines in your pet's eyes,
in that peace that inexplicably comes over you
at dawn, when the first inkling of light touches the Earth,
or dusk, when it recedes for the dawning of the next,
in the caring of human hearts when they help others.
There, every time, is God.

In every grace,
tragedy,
and healing,
God's love shines through it all.

In the illumination of the human soul,
for God is light,
God is love,
and all we ever need to do for ourselves is shine
as brightly as we can.

Our goal?
Our job here?
Our purpose?
To shine our light.
That is all.

An Offering | Returning What's Sacred

For if every human light bulb turned on
simultaneously,
at the exact precise moment,
there would no longer be darkness.
Not anywhere.
No darkness hiding in corners,
no darkness lingering,
no darkness to fear,
for the unified light shining as one
is the One,
shining through humanity.

This light,
your light,
is God's light.

God's love,
illuminating all creation.
And now, nothing
any longer
will be hidden.

So dear ones, shine.
Shine united in the four directions.
Turn your lights on
and illuminate the world.

For the good of all, and harm to none. *Aho!*

RESOURCES
Works Cited

"US Indian Boarding School History." *The National Native American Boarding School Healing Coalition*, -2020, boardingschoolhealing.org/education/us-indian-boarding-school-history/.

"Canada: 751 Unmarked Graves Found at Residential School." BBC, 24 Jun. 2021, www.bbc.com/news/world-us-canada-57592243.

Lindeman, Tracey. "Canada: Remains of 215 Children Found at Indigenous Residential School Site." *The Guardian,* 28 May 2021, www.theguardian.com/world/2021/may/28/canada-remains-indigenous-children-mass-graves.

Hopkins, Ruth. "Unmarked Graves at Indian Residential Schools Speak to Horrors Faced By Students." *Teen Vogue*, 14 Jul. 2021, www.teenvogue.com/story/indian-residential-schools-graves.

The Associated Press. "U.S. Report Identifies Burial Sites Linked to Boarding Schools for Native Americans." *National Public Radio,* 11 May 2022, www.npr.org/2022/05/11/1098276649/us-report-details-burial-sites-linked-to-boarding-schools-for-native-americans.

Coble, Christopher Esq. "If I Find an Eagle Feather, Can I Keep It?" *Find Law,* 21 Mar. 2019, www.findlaw.com/legalblogs/law-and-life/if-i-find-an-eagle-feather-can-i-keep-it/.

KMKENNEDY164. "The Funeral Practices of the Blackfoot and Cheyenne Tribes." *West of the Frontier: Death and Dying on the Great Plains,* 11 Feb. 2015, westofthefrontierdeathanddying.wordpress.com/2015/02/11/the-funeral-practices-of-the-blackfoot-and-cheyenne-tribes/.

"Swamp Yankee." *Wikipedia,* Wikimedia Foundation, 30 May 2023, en.wikipedia.org/wiki/Swamp_Yankee.

"Guards Accused of Unleashing Dogs, Pepper-spraying Oil Pipeline Protesters." *CBS News,* 5 Sept. 2016, www.cbsnews.com/news/dakota-access-pipeline-protest-turns-violent-in-north-dakota/.

Petronzio, Matt. "How Young Native Americans Built and Sustained the #NoDAPL Movement." *Mashable,* 7 Dec. 2016, mashable.com/article/standing-rock-nodapl-youth.

"A Conversation On The Sacred Stone Camp." *It's Going Down,* 4 Sept. 2016, itsgoingdown.org/conversation-on-sacred-stone-camp/.

"Standing Rock Historian on Pipeline Resistance." *Native Daily Network,* 5 Oct. 2016, nativedailynetwork.org/2016/10/05/standing-rock-historian-on-black-snake-fight/.

"Dakota Access Pipeline." *Dakota Access Pipeline,* 30 Jun. 2017, daplpipelinefacts.com/.

"Regulatory Tracker: The Dakota Access Pipeline (DAPL)." *Harvard University Environmental & Energy Law Program,* 8 Sept. 2023, eelp.law.harvard.edu/2017/10/dakota-access-pipeline/.

Wong, Julia C. "Police Remove Last Standing Rock Protesters in Military-style Takeover." *The Guardian,* 23 Feb. 2017, www.theguardian.com/us-news/2017/feb/23/dakota-access-pipeline-camp-cleared-standing-rock.

Janis, Red Fawn. "I'm Home and Ready To Keep Fighting." *Lakota Law,* 25 Mar. 2021, lakotalaw.org/news/2021-03-25/red-fawn-home-and-ready-to-fight.

"Standing Rock Water Protector Red Fawn Fallis Leaves Federal Prison." *Democracy Now!,* 11 Sept. 2020, www.democracynow.org/2020/9/11/headlines/standing_rock_water_protector_red_fawn_fallis_leaves_federal_prison.

Angeleti, Gabriella. "Massachusetts Museum Accused of Hoarding Indigenous Artifacts and Human Remains for Decades." *The Art Newspaper,* 1 Apr. 2022, www.theartnewspaper.com/2022/04/01/massachusetts-museum-accused-hoarding-indigenous-artefacts-human-remains.

Pratt, Mark. "Sacred Items in Barre Library's Museum to Be Returned to Sioux." *The Worcester Telegram & Gazette,* Associated Press, 11 Oct. 2022, www.telegram.com/story/news/2022/10/11/native-american-artifacts-barre-museum-returned-sioux/10463714002/.

Moreton, Bruce. "The Give Away Ceremony - a Lakota Tradition." *Night Eagle Wilderness Adventures,* 6 Nov. 2022, www.nighteaglewilderness.com/post/the-give-away-ceremony-a-lakota-tradition

Resources | Returning What's Sacred

More on Standing Rock

Gunderson, Dan. "'I Live with Standing Rock in My Heart': Massive Pipeline Protest Resonates 5 Years Later." *MPR News,* 1 Apr. 2021, www.mprnews.org/story/2021/04/01/i-live-with-standing-rock-in-my-heart-massive-pipeline-protest-resonates-5-years-later.

Clifton, Merritt. "Standing Rock: Who Let the Dogs Out?" *Animals 24-7,* 7 Sept. 2016, www.animals24-7.org/2016/09/07/standing-rock-who-let-the-dogs-out/.

"Dakota Access Pipeline Protests." *Wikipedia,* Wikimedia Foundation, 10 Sept. 2023, en.wikipedia.org/wiki/Dakota_Access_Pipeline_protests. Accessed 7 Oct. 2023.

The U.S Army Corps of Engineers originally considered a route north of Bismarck for the pipeline, but re-routed it closer to tribal lands, purportedly to reduce pipeline length by miles and dozens fewer crossings, but critics called the decision an example of environmental racism:

LaCapria, Kim. "DAPL Routed Through Standing Rock After Bismarck Residents Said No?" *Snopes,* 30 Nov. 2016, www.snopes.com/fact-check/dapl-routed-through-standing-rock-after-bismarck-residents-said-no/.

"Why a Previously Proposed Route for the Dakota Access Pipeline Was Rejected." *ABC News,* 3 Nov. 2016, abcnews.go.com/US/previously-proposed-route-dakota-access-pipeline-rejected/story?id=43274354.

Standing Rock, ND 2016-2017, see for reference: standwithstandingrock.net. Or watch: Awake, a Dream from Standing Rock at https://awakethefilm.org/

"Seven Fires Prophecy." *Wikipedia,* Wikimedia Foundation, 5 Oct. 2023, en.wikipedia.org/wiki/Seven_fires_prophecy. Accessed 7 Oct. 2023.

Pauls, Karen. "'We Must Kill the Black Snake': Prophecy and Prayer Motivate Standing Rock Movement." *CBC News,* 11 Dec. 2016, www.cbc.ca/news/canada/manitoba/dakota-access-pipeline-prayer-1.3887441.

Regan, Sheila. "'It's Cultural Genocide': Inside the Fight to Stop a Pipeline on Tribal Lands." *The Guardian,* 19 Feb. 2021, www.theguardian.com/us-news/2021/feb/19/line-3-pipeline-ojibwe-tribal-lands.

Kesel, Aaron. "Native American Protesters Banned from Protesting on Their Own Land." *We Are Change,* 22 Aug. 2016, wearechange.org/native-american-protesters-banned/.

Levin, Sam. "'He's a Political Prisoner': Standing Rock Activists Face Years in Jail." *The Guardian,* 22 Jun. 2018, www.theguardian.com/us-news/2018/jun/22/standing-rock-jailed-activists-water-protectors.

Janis, Red Fawn. "I'M Home and Ready To Keep Fighting." *Lakota Law,* 25 Mar. 2021, lakotalaw.org/news/2021-03-25/red-fawn-home-and-ready-to-fight.

"Standing Rock Water Protector Red Fawn Fallis Leaves Federal Prison." *Democracy Now!,* 11 Sept. 2020, www.democracynow.org/2020/9/11/headlines/standing_rock_water_protector_red_fawn_fallis_leaves_federal_prison.

Recommended Reading

Violet H. Catches, *Xeyata*

Marie Dion, *Journey of a Red Soul*

Isabelle Knockwood, *Out of the Depths: The Experiences of Mi'kmaw Children at the Indian Residential School at Shubenacadie, Nova Scotia*

Diane Wilson, *Beloved Child: A Dakota Way of Life*

Diane Wilson, *The Seed Keeper*

Winona LaDuke, *Recovering the Sacred*

On Wounded Knee: https://www.khanacademy.org/humanities/us-history/the-gilded-age/american-west/a/ghost-dance-and-wounded-knee

Don Miguel Ruiz, *The Four Agreements*

Dr. Clarissa Pinkola Estes, *Women Who Run with the Wolves*

Wab Kinew, *The Reason You Walk*

Tosha Silver, *Outrageous Openness: Letting the Divine Take the Lead*

Don Miguel Ruiz, *The Four Agreements*

Kent Nerburn, *Voices in the Stones: Life Lessons from the Native Way*

Joan Grant, *Many Lifetimes*

Helen Knott, *In My Own Moccasins—A Memoir of Resilience*

ACKNOWLEDGMENTS

Thank you to my patient best friend and business partner Charisse Sisou. How do I describe her relationship to this book? Part editor, part midwife, part coach, all soul sister. *Returning What's Sacred* would never have seen the light of day without her. Thank you, from the deepest place in my heart.

So much gratitude to the dear friends, family, and cultural mentors who read and reviewed earlier iterations of this book: Violet H. Catches, Keith Chiefmoon, Roberta Greany, Sandi Isgro, Yvonne Romiglio, and Willow Daly. Your insights, input and feedback made this book so much clearer and stronger. *Wela'lin.*

Thank you to all of the many people who, knowingly or unknowingly, played a role in the return of the sacred object to its home in the Black Hills of South Dakota, and all that unfolded as a result, especially Kelly Two Wolves, Stephanie Kenny and Mary Tomassetti. Without you, White Wolf's pipe would never have found its resting place, and I, my healing and growth. Your contributions were instrumental on this journey. And to all those too many to name, you know who you are. I am truly grateful for all of you.

Emset Nogemag

ABOUT THE AUTHOR
Marie Dion

Author and speaker Marie Dion brings forward the messages of her ancestors through her life experiences. Her pen name honors the legacy of her great-great-grandmother Marie, who hid her Native identity to protect her children from being taken away and put into residential schools.

An award-winning graphic designer, published author, versatile artist, and spiritual channel, Marie's ancestral heritage melds Blackfoot, Wolastoqiyik (Maliseet), and Mi'kmaq descent with French Canadian and Italian. She bridges cultures and artistic mediums as well as the tangible and intangible with a unique ability to tap into the unseen world.

Learn more about her at MarieDion.com

Don't miss the acclaimed book by Marie Dion:

JOURNEY OF A RED SOUL

Journey of a Red Soul is the story of Marie's life as told by her ancestors, who showed her how the events and relationships of her current life related to past lives, like puzzle pieces snapping into place: one soul, one journey, many lives.

Born into an Italian, Catholic family in the 1960s, Marie did not delve into her First Nations ancestry until she was in her thirties. Once she did, the threads of her early mystical experiences, inexplicable reactions to ordinary things, and ability to remember past lifetimes began to come together to reveal her role as a bridge between worlds.

The book traces Marie's path of discovery, sharing lessons and insights learned in previous Native lifetimes toward healing racism of all forms: namely, that we are all interconnected and "walk in the other's shoes."

"Marie Dion has penned a story that brings to life one person's search for place, identity, and origins." —W. Michael Gear, NYT Bestselling Author

"Our country needs to heal its past with the First People for us all to prosper… This book is a courageous step in that process."
—Lisa Campion, Author and Psychic Counselor

To learn more, visit mariedion.com

www.ingramcontent.com/pod-product-compliance
Lightning Source LLC
Chambersburg PA
CBHW061735070526
44585CB00024B/2679